The Hard Work Series Presents

THE HARD WORK OF HAPPINESS

A guide to living a life of
pleasure, purpose & meaning

REB BUXTON

The Hard Work of Happiness:
A Guide To Living A Life
of Pleasure, Purpose & Meaning

Copyright © 2018 Reb Buxton
All rights reserved.

No part of this book may be reproduced in any form or by any electronic or mechanical means, including information storage and retrieval systems, without permission in writing from the publisher, except by reviewers, who may quote brief passages in a review.

This book is not intended as a substitute for the counseling advice from a trained psychotherapist. The reader should consult a professional in matters relating to his/her mental health and particularly with respect to any symptoms that may require diagnosis or medical attention.

ISBN 978-1-7323788-2-7

Design and illustrations by Tim Delger
Printed in the United States of America
Published by The Flow Farm Press
810 Dominican Drive
Nashville, TN 37228
www.TheFlowFarm.com
Visit the author's website at www.RebBuxton.com

*Until you make your unconscious conscious,
it will direct your life and you will call it fate.*

- Carl Jung

*Do I contradict myself? Very well, then
I contradict myself, I am large, I contain
multitudes.*

- Walt Whitman

the only thing I can really learn is how to be content with myself knowing

Art installation imbedded in the ground of Center Camp at Burning Man 2017

This book is dedicated to my sister, Debbie, whose parts are constantly seeking happiness...just like all of us.

Contents

Foundations

Introduction 3

Beginning 11

Stacking–Part 1 31

Stacking–Part 2 39

The Cycle of Self-Determination 47

The Footstool & The Clocktower 59

Enneagram 65

Attachment 77

Internal Family Systems 83

The 8 C's

The 8 C's 107

Compassion vs. Apathy 111

Compassion in Action 121

Calm vs. Chaos 135

Curiosity vs. Arrogance 145

Courage vs. Cowardice 153

Connected vs. Lonely 163

Creativity vs. Rigidity 173

Confidence vs. Insecurity 181

Clarity vs. Confusion 191

Clarity 199

Tools

Relationships–Part 1 209

Relationships–Part 2 221

Anxiety–Part 1 231

Anxiety–Part 2 247

Facing Your Fears 253

Young Man/Old Man 259

S.T.A.R. 267

AUTHOR'S NOTE

I am among the fortunate who can answer with confidence the age-old question of "Why am I here?" It is my profound privilege and purpose to help others learn how to alleviate unnecessary suffering. By doing so, what is left is sacred, and sacred suffering has a purpose. If we must suffer, and we all must, then let us suffer well and together. By suffering well, we write new endings to our painful stories. Through this intentional act of rewriting our history, we redeem those lonely, dark nights of despair into stories of resilience. As we heal, the love we are given and the love we give become the ultimate, defining purpose of life, filling our cups to overflowing with gratitude and joy. May your life be rid of all unnecessary suffering and may it be filled with an abundance of compassion, calmness, courage, creativity, clarity, connectedness, confidence and curiosity. May you free yourself from unnecessary burdens and wrestle well with your sacred suffering and find authentic happiness.

PART I

FOUNDATIONS

I

INTRODUCTION

On the corner of High Street and Wall Street in New Haven, Connecticut, sits an austere art deco building erected in 1963. In this building are housed some of the rarest manuscripts in the world. The Beinecke Rare Book & Manuscript Library is, as Robert A. M. Stern, Dean of the Yale School of Architecture, describes it "one of the great treasure houses of Yale."

One of the library's strange yet alluring features is the soaring central book tower with more than 180,000 rare titles. This monolith inside a monolith stands as a tribute to the history of the written word. Beneath it in the underground book stacks are one million more unusual manuscripts nestled comfortably in temperature- and humidity-controlled rooms.

Sitting undisturbed most days in another climate-controlled chamber filed under the uninteresting designation MS 408 is a 272-page manuscript that serves as one of the greatest literary mysteries in history. The Voynich manuscript, named after the Polish book dealer Wilfrid Voynich who purchased the item in 1912, is a codex written in the early 1400s most likely in a small village in northern Italy. The actual text is written in an elegant but unknown language. Professional and amateur cryptographers alike have poured over the text, and each and every one have met the same fate. Even the famed American and British code breakers, including National Security Agency (NSA) experts, have been unable to unlock its mystery.

Theories abound as to the origin and meaning of the text. Some believe it to be a hoax. Some say it may have been inspired by extraterrestrials. Others believe it may be incoherent religious ramblings manifested during free writing sessions or glossolalia experiences. Still others think it is a simple encryption system that was adapted and augmented by adding meaningless and duplicate symbols, false word breaks and the transposition of letters. Whatever the case, the mystery still stands.

Historically speaking, writing and decoding secret messages goes back many thousands of years to 1900 BCE from a period known as the *Old Kingdom of Egypt*.[1] These "non-standard" hieroglyphics carved into the walls and tombs were the first known attempts to disguise a message using secret codes and encryptions. It is believed that these were meant more for mystery and intrigue than passing secrets,

---

1 https://en.wikipedia.org/wiki/History_of_cryptography

INTRODUCTION

but they were coded messages nonetheless. Today cryptography and cryptanalysis are big business with nations, armies, terrorist organizations and businesses attempting to protect (or steal) trade secrets.

Everyone loves the intrigue of mysteries and secrets. It may be a secret handshake between best friends in 4th grade or the cutesy phrases lovers whisper to one another in public knowing no one else will understand. It is our penchant for privacy that attracts us to secrecy.

In every field of inquiry man has created to understand this fascinating and bizarre world, unsolved mysteries abound that puzzle the best and brightest among us. This includes the field of brain science.

Advances in neuroscience and technology have provided us with lifesaving innovations and a profound understanding of the structure of the brain that were unimaginable even a hundred years ago. One example of this extraordinary ability to map the brain is that we now know our brain has approximately 86 billion neurons. Each single neuron makes up to 40,000 connections, resulting in trillions of connections. As a point of reference there are about 100 billion stars in the Milky Way galaxy. The cosmic joke is that despite our profound insights and scientific advances, each and every new baby born is another Voynich manuscript cloaked in mystery.

It is as if each person's brain is a secret text full of profound mysteries that we cannot fully fathom. Yet this lone organ is the final arbiter in how we think, how we act and each decision we make. Science and religion offer a fair amount of guidance and wisdom to help us navigate the world, but ultimately everything we experience must first pass through our brain. In one sense we are held captive to the capacities and abilities of our brains. We cannot get outside of ourselves, and no one can join us in the inner sanctum of our mind.

What you will discover in the following pages are specific and practical ways to understand how your brain/mind system, including your conscious and unconscious, are configured. Once you better understand these powerful, dynamic structures, you will have a greater appreciation for how your brain receives, translates and interprets information.

Whenever we are given knowledge, we are actually being given the power of choice. We have the right to do a lot with this new information or nothing at all. For those who choose the courageous path of self-discovery, all of life becomes a resplendent adventure to understanding the mystery of who we are, why we are here and why we do what we do. As you do this good, hard work, life will reward you with joy, meaning, play, love and, yes, authentic happiness.

We all have issues that we have been struggling with for a very long time, sometimes years. These will often feel impossible to solve. We have tried everything we know to do, yet they keep returning like an army of cockroaches. "Impossible problems" rarely, if ever, have easy,

INTRODUCTION

straightforward answers. Here are a few examples of life's impossible problems:

- Should I leave my troubled marriage or stay for the children?

- Why do I keep dating (and breaking up with) the same type of person?

- Why do I have this non stop brain filled with anxiety that prevents me from enjoying my life?

- I hate my job, but I don't know what to do. I'm not trained to do anything else. I'm married now and have kids. It's too late for me to go back to school.

Decoding the mystery of who you are is hard work. No one gives you an owner's manual of how to be a successful adult and live a happy life. You have to figure out a lot on your own. If you want to jump to the head of the line, you must explore what is going on beneath the surface of your conscious, day-to-day awareness.

This book makes two assumptions. First is that you have two minds. One of those minds is conscious, and the other is unconscious. The unconscious is more powerful, yet its fatal flaw is that it lacks conscious awareness, hence the need for the less powerful, more nimble conscious mind. The more you understand the interplay between your unconscious and conscious mind, the greater your ability to positively, thoughtfully and intentionally create the life you want. Imagine two people rowing a boat. If they are not working together, or worse, working against each other, they will not make much progress. Once they begin to work together, they can zoom across the lake. As a note, a more realistic comparison in this boating metaphor would be that the conscious mind is the boat, paddles and people who are in the boat and the unconscious is the enormous lake upon which they are floating.

It is incorrect to think that information flows only one way from your unconscious to your conscious mind. There is a deep interplay between the two. For example, most of us don't think much about *how* our personality is constructed. We automatically respond to stimuli according to what we think will make us happy. But just because you don't typically examine a particular feature of your unconsciously driven personality doesn't mean you can't.

Directing focused attention at a particular aspect of your personality (e.g., the tendency to go to anger too quickly, perfectionism, people pleasing, worrying, etc.) can significantly improve this trait and as a result improve your lives. It is true that what you focus on will flourish. This is one example of how the conscious mind can influence the unconscious.

The same is true when you understand how you attach to others. If you are aware of your attachment style and that of your partner and how those two dynamics interact early on in the dating dance, you will better understand how both of you will act in moments of stress. For example, someone with an avoidant attachment will need more time alone to process and feel calm than an anxious or securely attached individual. Once you are aware of this, you can choose what you are willing to tolerate or not. Even this one insight can be the difference between living

INTRODUCTION

a long, happy life together or enduring a marriage filled with constant disappointment and misery.

The second assumption is that your mind is, for all practical purposes, infinitely complex and therefore must operate in multiplicity. This simply means that your mind is made up of parts known as subpersonalities. Each part has its own thoughts and opinions that often disagree with other parts, thereby creating internal stress. This explains simply and elegantly how you can hold many opposing thoughts and ideas on the same topic without being psychotic. Each part wants what it believes is best for you. It has strong opinions about how to manifest those desires. Sometimes when various parts disagree with each other, the relationship becomes hostile. Anyone forced to participate in a dysfunctional group can appreciate how difficult it can be to get anything done when there isn't a healthy synergy among the members. One way to create a healthy mind is to build a bridge of understanding among your parts that will allow them to share their perspectives and communicate effectively. This is one way to jump to the head of the line when it comes to being happy in love and life.

By the time you finish this book, you will have a fundamental understanding of the systems at work in your unconscious. This information will help you decipher much faster and with more sophistication your thoughts, feelings, behaviors and motivations. This information will help you solve those impossible problems more effectively, but more importantly, it will help prevent many of them from occurring in the first place. This is what everyday happiness looks like.

2
—

BEGINNING

The most widely known precept of Buddhism is that suffering is a fact of life that cannot be avoided. Efforts to ignore, suppress or deny the inevitable ironically create suffering that is unnecessary. At first glance, this notion that life is suffering seems a dismal proposition. However, below its surface is wise instruction: To live a happy life you must decide what is worth suffering for and how to suffer well.

The reality is that we all end up in complex life dramas with twists and turns we could never have imagined or anticipated. Many times we begin a new journey with the best of intentions only to have the whole thing unravel. Tragedy befalls each and every one of us. Most of us can accept that sometimes things don't work out in our favor. Ask Floyd Horn about losing $380 million by missing the winning lottery ticket by one number. What must it have been like for Kevin Pearce to be a favorite for the gold medal in his first Olympics only to suffer a career-ending injury weeks before opening ceremonies?

These events are breathtaking in their misfortune. Most of the struggles we face on a day-to-day basis are nowhere near this magnitude. But our tragedies are still important. Just because someone may have suffered more than we have does not diminish our suffering or make it less important.

This book is based on a set of optimistic ideas, all of which seek to help you understand how to alleviate unnecessary suffering and how to embrace sacred suffering. One of those ideas is the straightforward principle that staying too long in a bad thing is a bad thing that leads to other bad things and prevents good things from happening. The key phrase here is *too long.* No one intentionally chooses suffering. It is more often thrust on us against our will. But we can choose to walk away from "a bad thing" once we see it's no good. If we don't walk away from a bad thing, we are inviting unnecessary suffering. When we do walk away, we open a space in our hearts and minds for something better to enter.

I am convinced that everything we do is to make ourselves happy. It is probably more accurate to say that our actions, at any given moment, are for the express purpose of making some part of ourselves happy. This does not mean that the action itself is enjoyable. A soldier training to be a Navy SEAL might be getting thrashed, but he knows that if he survives the training and becomes a SEAL, that will make him extremely happy and proud.

To say that everything we do is to make ourselves happy is controversial. However, consider for a moment the last few activities you engaged in before sitting down to read this book. Did you kiss your children and tuck them in bed? Eat a salad? Pour yourself a glass of wine? Ask an attractive girl at your gym out on a date? Scroll through Instagram, Tinder or Facebook? Do you see the common thread of happiness in all these activities?

Granted, many times our efforts to achieve happiness are gambles that do not pay off. You are not certain that reading this book will make you happier, but you are willing to take the chance. Why? Because in and of itself, taking the chance of learning new ideas that could bring you closer to the type of happiness you seek makes you happy.

I spent considerable time formulating the title of this book. Here are a few that ended up on the cutting room floor: What To Do With Impossible Problems, Winning The Unconscious Game, The Last Self-Help Book You'll Ever Need (egotistical I know) and Thriving In Chaos. So why did I land on *The Hard Work Of Happiness?* First, I think true happiness is underappreciated, yet it motivates everything we do. From skipping stones at the lake with your children to helping build freshwater wells for villages in poverty-stricken countries halfway around the world, it is all about making ourselves happy. Second, personally and professionally, I have found achieving lasting, authentic happiness to be literally hard work.

But wait! Aren't we warned that pursuing happiness is shallow at best and self-centered and hedonistic at worst? Many consider happiness a second-rate, ephemeral state that is acceptable only occasionally but should not be thought of as permanent. Shouldn't we pursue joy, love, meaningfulness and altruism instead?

If happiness is confined to a superficial feeling while experiencing something pleasurable, then yes, it would be foolish to order one's life around such simplemindedness. Because our hedonic tendencies are insatiable, they constantly roam for something new, novel and strange. The happiness we extract from our material possessions inevitably fades over time, leaving a void that we then fill with more stuff. If this statement is true, then why would anyone pay ridiculous amounts of money for expensive luxury items that will only provide temporary satisfaction? You guessed it: Because it makes them happy!

However, happiness, like love, is polysemous. The ancient Greeks had a different view on what constitutes happiness. They didn't eschew the idea of happiness, they embraced it, deepened it. Aristotle, specifically, delineated multiple dimensions of happiness.

In *Nicomachean Ethics*, Aristotle sought to discover "the supreme good for man." What is the best way for a person to live? Aristotle believed our motivations were similar to animals in many ways but different in one very important way: the ability to reason and to use that reason to pursue happiness. Happiness, he suggests, is not a goal to be achieved but an ongoing activity that must be pursued with thoughtfulness and reason. He believed in a "middle way" of living between extremes of excess and deprivation. Therefore, happiness is a virtuous action continually cultivated by habit of behaviors that emphasize pleasure, wisdom, courage, self-discipline and altruism.

Martin Seligman, the founding father of Positive Psychology, updated Aristotle's ideas for modern times. In his groundbreaking work, Seligman observed how psychology focused primarily on moving people from a negative ten up to zero. This, he surmised, is a worthy goal, and psychology, psychiatry and psychotherapy all made worthy contributions to humanity by reducing suffering. Seligman, however, had a more ambitious challenge: Why not try to move people from zero to positive ten?

Seligman proposed the idea that to live a happy life we need to expand the idea of what being happy means. Basing his theory on Aristotle's *Ethics*, Seligman described three ways of living: *The Pleasurable Life, The Good Life & The Meaningful Life*. Taken in this context, happiness is less one-dimensional and more dynamic.

The Pleasurable Life is based on sensorial pleasures of both body and mind. Think of sitting in the warm sun at the beach listening to the waves crash against the shore. Think of enjoying an exquisite meal with dear friends before heading off to the movies together. Think of getting a massage at your favorite spa before going to the salon for a makeover. These are all examples of *The Pleasurable Life*.

The Good Life is characterized by courage and curiosity. Living *The Good Life* means perpetually seeking to learn and understand one's self and others, finding purpose in life through meaningful work and acting with integrity when facing fears. *The Good Life* seeks adventure through greater self-awareness but also by taking literal adventures to engage the world outside of the typically safe and predictable routines of daily life. One defining characteristic of *The Good Life* is what the Japanese call ikigai. This threefold path involves discovering what you are good at doing, what you find the most pleasure in doing and what others will pay you to do. Once you discover your strengths, you then fashion your life in such a way as to manifest flow states or what the Greeks called eudemonia or human flourishing. As Fabienne Fredrickson noted, "The things you are passionate about are not random, they are your calling."

Finally, *The Meaningful Life* is inclusive of all that *The Pleasurable Life* and *The Good Life* have to offer. However, *The Meaningful Life* moves beyond the ego and takes all the manifested goodness of *The Pleasurable Life* and the wisdom of the *The Good Life* and gives back to others. By giving out of your abundance, you create a positive loop of gratitude that cycles back and forth between you and the person you are serving. You get your deepest needs met and contribute your unique passions, gifts and talents to those who can benefit from them. As theologian Frederick Buechner writes, "Your vocation in life is where your greatest joy meets the world's greatest need." Through your struggles, failures and victories, you are privileged to be able to help others on their journey.

Our very own *Declaration of Independence* contains important ideas on happiness, "We hold these truths to be self-evident, that all men are created equal and that they are endowed by their Creator with certain unalienable rights: that among these are life, liberty, and the pursuit of happiness."

—

If happiness is one of the bedrock motivations and foundations of our democracy, then why are we, as a country, so unhappy?

Surgeon General Sylvia Trent-Adams recently posted on her official Twitter account, "Loneliness is associated with increased risk of premature death. And the effect on mortality is comparable to [sic] impact of smoking or obesity."

Loneliness? How could such an advanced culture that is connected every minute of the day with everything and everyone be so fundamentally lonely? Part of the problem is due to information overload. I don't need to argue for how dependent we have become on mobile devices, the internet, on-demand programming, etc.

Another factor in the epidemic of loneliness is the fast-paced nature of modern life. Because we can work from home every third Thursday and wear jeans on Friday, we are expected to be available to solve any problem that crops up at work at any moment. Our managers know we are rarely if ever more than an arm's length away from our smartphones.

Sometimes we are tempted to play the role of a super hero who can solve work problems on the go while dropping off the kids at soccer practice before dashing over for a quick trip to the grocery store before driving back across town to pick up the kids to make it home in time to cook dinner (women especially in our culture are expected to maintain a seamless transition between their professional and domestic roles), then have quality time with our partner so we can get up and do the whole rat race over again tomorrow. That is exhausting just to write. It used to take a village to raise a family (or at least a cluster of family members from different generations who all lived nearby). Now it is supposed to take two people…and sometimes only one. Could this be a clue as to why we are sliding down the happiness scale?

There is research showing that it's not just us adults who are less happy. From 1991–2016 there have been an analysis of one million 8th, 10th and 12th graders on subjective well-being—the clinical term for happiness. Since the introduction of smartphones, teenagers have shown a marked decline in happiness[1] with a sharp decline in 2012. What happened? More screen time and less non-phone-related activities. To be fair, the happiest kids were those who had some screen time mixed with other activities.

There are other factors. We are a consumer-driven culture that promises the next purchase will make us "happy." Our brains are wired to seek pleasure (happiness), and when we buy something, even when we can't afford it, we do it because it makes us happy for a moment. The biological motivation behind this retail therapy is the rush of the happiness chemicals—dopamine, serotonin, oxytocin and endorphins—we experience when getting something

---

1 http://psycnet.apa.org/doiLanding?doi=10.1037%2Femo0000403

new. In other words: Retail therapy is a drug that makes us happy...for a moment.

Our brains crave this chemical wash. Like rats in the lab who can't stop hitting the lever for a sugar pellet, we are programmed for pleasure when we get a new phone, watch, outfit, car, computer, coffee, boyfriend, girlfriend, husband, wife, etc.

Buddhist philosophy teaches that life is suffering, everything changes and *nothing* fully satisfies. If nothing, *nothing* fully satisfies, then why not chase whatever glimmers of happiness we can find in the moment? Isn't it our inalienable right to be happy? Though few people would outwardly admit it, many of us live our lives in just such a way.

Another factor that blocks us from happiness is worrying about things beyond our control. According to a study conducted by the Mayo Clinic and the National Institute on Aging, seventy percent of Americans are on prescription drugs. Americans are number one in the world in terms of how many people take medications as well as how many medications each person takes. Yet from data published in 2016 by the World Health Organization, we rank 31st in life expectancy. The main reason for this is obesity. Could there be a more revealing marker for a one-dimensional view of happiness than obesity? Shoving high-calorie, low-quality food into our pie holes at a faster rate than our sedentary, technology-obsessed lifestyle can burn off is a morbid picture of our lack of creativity and enthusiasm for a meaningful life.

Obesity has many causes that disadvantage certain populations, such as poverty and genetics. If you are born into poverty and have a family history of Type 2 diabetes, the cards are stacked against you before you're even born. But that doesn't account for the nearly forty percent rate of obesity in our country. We just want to feel happy, even if it is only for a moment and it costs us our future health. These discouraging statistics go on and on. We are 44th when it comes to infant mortality, yet we supposedly have the most sophisticated (and complicated) health system in the world.

We are a suffering nation, and most of the suffering is unnecessary. We so desperately want to be happy but subject ourselves day after day to one horrible, divisive news story after another. We need to be connected to other people but are afraid of that person next to us in the grocery store checkout line. Television shows like *To Catch A Predator* erode our confidence in humanity as the stream of servicemen, police officers, judges, teachers, priests or high school coaches are caught in the act of luring a child into having sex. These prey on our deepest fears, so we choose to trust no one. As a result, we are disconnected from others, which ultimately disconnects us from ourselves.

—

Let's return to the unconscious. We have many systems that run automatically behind the scenes. They keep our heart beating and food digesting. They sort and store our memories and process data from the external world based on our personality, attachment style and our many subpersonalities.

But what happens when trauma disrupts the normal operation of the psyche? None of us would be able to manage a single day if we could not suppress our traumatic memories. We would be reduced to a puddle of tears unable to complete basic ADLs (Activities of Daily Living). We admit people to psychiatric hospitals who cannot suppress their trauma enough to function normally in life.

Where, then, do these traumatic memories go? We have many strategies for repressing painful memories. We can refuse to process them. We can pretend they never happened. We can suppress them by overindulging in vices. We can project them onto other people. Each of these works to a lesser or greater degree until something or someone triggers them. Once triggered, these terrible memories come back with a vengeance, full of anger at being ignored. Many times these memories resurface in unexpected ways and at inconvenient times through anxiety attacks, sudden outbursts of anger, fear and/or debilitating sadness and depression.

However terrible the experience of revisiting our trauma may be, the truth is life must go on regardless. We must perform at work, at home, with children, with friends and romantic partners. Though we may not consciously be aware of how deeply affected we are on a minute-to-minute basis, our wounds continue to be processed in our unconscious. The purpose of this continual wound analysis is to set up internal fortifications to prevent ever getting traumatized in the same way again.

If at any point we experience something remotely similar to what caused us so much pain, our unconscious will sound the alarm in an attempt to ward off the threat. If we don't get the message or don't respond to it in the way our unconscious thinks is safe, it will up the ante with panic or dread. Maybe we hear a song that triggers a memory or see someone who looks eerily similar to the person who harmed us. The cascade of internal warnings will continue to intensify until we remove ourselves from the danger. If we don't act on our "flight" response (e.g., stay in an abusive relationship), then our system will wage war against itself that inevitably leads to depression, anxiety or worse.

In this state of internal unrest we don't find relationships as interesting. Food is bland and uninteresting. We stay in bed all weekend. We isolate ourselves because going outside takes so much energy, and we want to protect those we care about from our misery. We fear our depression is a virus that might infect others. We medicate with food, alcohol and TV to escape. We troll social media as a form of self-mutilation with all of its sparkling images that make our muted existence pale in comparison. We logically understand we need to ask for help but from whom and for what? This is the fertile ground upon which impossible problems take root.

People don't bring their easy problems to therapy. They bring impossible problems. Impossible problems feel impossible because all attempts to solve them have come up short. Our only options seem to range from bad to worse. The very nature of impossible problems is that they are not static. The problems themselves shift and change on a regular basis. The solutions we came up with yesterday don't work today. Like an enemy combatant who changes their tactics to evade defeat, so too do our impossible problems adjust based on our efforts to solve them. That is why our strategies for solving these longstanding challenges must be adaptive as well.

Timothy Keller makes a sobering observation in *Walking With God Through Pain and Suffering*:

> No matter what precautions we take, no matter how well we have put together a good life, no matter how hard we have worked to be healthy, wealthy, and comfortable with friends and family, and successful with our career—something will inevitably ruin it. No amount of money, power, and planning can prevent bereavement, dire illness, relationship betrayal, financial disaster, or a host of troubles from entering your life. Human life is fatally fragile and subject to forces beyond our power to manage. Life is tragic. We all know this intuitively, and those who face the challenges of suffering and pain learn all too well that it is impossible to do so using our own resources. We all need support if we are not to succumb to despair.

The support we need may come through traditional methods such as asking for help from friends and family, psychotherapy, medications, books, support groups, religious affiliation, etc. There is, however, a less conventional way of experiencing healing via what I refer to as *The Universe*.

I use *The Universe* as a way to describe whatever benevolent force is behind the mysteriously arranged events of our life. I ascribe the feminine pronoun *She* to *The Universe* not on an ontological or politically correct basis. I do so for a more practical reason: When I interact with *The Universe*, it feels familiar and feminine to me. Hence the descriptor *She* seems appropriate.

Whether you believe in a benevolent force at work in *The Universe* or not, I think we can all admit that there are moments when something happens that is beyond explanation. If you have not experienced these, it is because you are not paying attention. It does not matter where you think these events originated or to whom you ascribe them. They are beyond our ability to understand. It only matters that you find the humility to receive them as gifts and be grateful. I have discovered that in these moments *The Universe* is trying to give us something we need and/or want.

When I attempt to explain to clients the role I feel *The Universe* plays in their search for happiness, I use the image of a scale. On one side of the scale are stacked all the healthy decisions they make, both big or small. In my imagination these are represented by gold coins. These could be grand gestures like donating millions of dollars to helping with medical care in poverty-stricken areas of the world. These acts could also be more intimate in nature like picking up a piece of trash in a city park.

On the other side of this scale are the unhealthy decisions represented by lead coins. Again these may be bad decisions on an epic scale such as the atrocities committed by malevolent dictators against their own people in an effort to retain power and suppress freedom. They may also seem benign like tossing a cigarette butt out the window of your car.

It may seem as if I am oversimplifying life and that if we just do good things, good things will happen, and if we do bad things, bad things will happen. However, what I witness in my own life and the lives of clients is something far more involved and personal.

The reality is that good things happen to bad people and bad things happen to good people. Things that make no sense happen to us all. The scale analogy begins to wobble under the lightest of scrutiny. Yet what I have observed is that *The Universe* is very patient. Just because the scale on the tip of her finger may have more coins stacked on one side or the other doesn't mean the scale will actually tip in that direction. She does not work on our timelines or our logic.

My observation is that She is very patient, giving us countless opportunities to turn our ship around and make good, healthy (often hard) decisions. When She chooses to act in our lives, it is motivated by love. Sometimes her gifts are generous. Other times they feel harsh and punitive. Either way they are what we need for that moment. We can choose to receive her wisdom or reject it at our own risk.

There are so many caveats to what I just wrote I can almost hear your eyes rolling, dear reader. "What about the time my mother got cancer when I was eleven and my father abandoned us for another woman and her kids and my teenage brother had to raise us?" I don't know. I don't understand that either. And I am truly sorry that happened to you. Life is not fair. "What about the mothers and fathers and children who are starving and suffering in war-torn areas of the world? Is your *Universe* 'loving' them too?" I don't know. I don't understand either. And I'm truly sorry it is happening. Life is not fair.

The only thing I am certain of is that I have front-row seats to the most incredible show on earth: the intimate, private lives of my clients. Every day I am privileged, grateful and humbled to witness their struggles and successes. Their stories are filled with magic and tragedy, which often happen in very close proximity to one another. I often see a faint outline on the edges of what I call *The Universe* at play.

What I believe is that throughout every day, each of us encounters what I call "magic moments." These magic moments are opportunities to make choices that stack either a gold coin on the healthy side of our scale or a lead coin on the unhealthy side. At some point for reasons unknown, *The Universe* chooses to act. As we move into and through these opportunities, something may happen based on our actions or nothing may happen, but in our hearts and minds and on our scales it is noted.

Here is a story that illustrates *The Universe* sprinkling some of her fairy dust in one of my therapy sessions. Once I had a client who was also a therapist. She and I worked together for over a year through a very difficult time in her life. We both knew our time was coming to a close, but neither of us was ready to make the call just yet.

After working with someone for a year, you get to know them pretty well. So I was surprised when at the beginning of a session she shared with me something I didn't know about her past, which was her receiving a scholarship to play sports in college.

After telling me her story, I closed my eyes and jokingly put my pen to my forehead as if I were a psychic and said, "Let me see if I can guess your jersey number." When I did this, two numbers came to mind: 7 and 10. I told her I couldn't tell if it was seven or if it was ten. A look of shock and disbelief came over her face. I was concerned and confused.

"What's wrong?" I asked

"How did you know that?" she finally managed to say.

"I...don't know. Why?"

She went on to tell me this story.

Her father, whom she dearly loves, had also received a scholarship to play baseball in college. When he played his number was ten. As a tribute to his positive influence in her life, she wanted to be number ten. Unfortunately, that number was already taken by another teammate. So instead she chose number seven. When her teammate eventually graduated, she switched her number from seven to ten.

Now I was the one dumbstruck by what had just occurred.

"Well, that's weird," was all I could think to say.

"Uh…yeah," she said laughing.

This experience had no obvious impact on the course of our counseling. Then why am I telling this story? There are two reasons why I feel this story is relevant.

First, it is a practical example of the power of *The Universe* playfully weaving herself into small moments in important ways. The probability of guessing one jersey number is very high. The complexity of the story multiplies many times with the addition of two jersey numbers. The reason is that most college athletes never change their jersey number as long as they play. I am no mathematician, but the probability of guessing she had not one but two jersey numbers *and* guessing both of them correctly seems extremely unlikely.

Another important factor is that this was the first time she and I had ever discussed this topic. The reason I am so certain of this is because when I envision a female softball player, I typically imagine a strong woman with a stocky build. My client weighed maybe 100 pounds now and weighed even less in college. This visual non sequitur of her diminutive stature and my stereotypical image of a female softball player's physique made an impression on me.

The second reason why this story is important is its longevity. I am still talking about it to this day. It is as if *The Universe* gifted me with a way to talk about her strange phenomenon in a confident, humorous, quirky way. *The Universe* has a serious dark side as well. Just look at any of the impossible problems you are struggling with today. But I also think She is also telling us that in our struggles She can be playful.

The best answer I have been able to muster from the pain I have endured, caused and observed, all the training, healing and redemption I have witnessed and experienced is that the authentic happiness we seek lies in our ability to make meaning from the terrific *and* the terrible. Our ability to find the fortune in the misfortune. Our capacity to love others and ourselves and make better choices where our lives flow in a healthier direction. Once we begin to see the obstacle in front of us as the way forward, not something to be avoided and discarded, we will thrive in spite of any temporary circumstances.

Today you have a choice. Will you face your challenges? Your character flaws? Your pain? Will you own the pain you have caused others and seek reconciliation? The secret to a successful life is a challenging but rewarding road not for the faint of heart and not without failing often. As Samuel Beckett wrote in *Worstward Ho*, "Ever tried. Ever failed. No matter. Try again. Fail again. Fail better."

3
—

STACKING – PART I

If I had to summarize in one sentence a single practice for finding true happiness it would be this: Through sheer power of will, discipline and grit, combined with a clear sense of personal values and moral conviction, make a perpetual habit of stacking one good decision on top of the other all day every day. Eventually you will find flow. Opportunities will manifest. This habit will prevent many problems from occurring in the first place. In this constellation of positivity a sense of well-being and true happiness will flourish.

Stacking requires a certain kind of sacred suffering. In many situations you will be required to do the thing you don't want to do and not do the thing you want to do. Evidence of this can be found throughout any given day. Stay in bed or get up and exercise? Order the large drink and fries at lunch or take the extra ten minutes before leaving for work to fix yourself a salad for lunch (and don't forget to drink a glass of water)? Don't buy the latest and greatest electronic gizmo. Instead, refurbish the one you already own. What do you get if you exercise, eat healthy and save money over time? Better health and less debt, which will eventually lead to more freedom and the ability to enjoy that freedom. Navy SEAL Jocko Willink summarizes this idea in three words: Discipline equals freedom. Stacking is a fundamental property of true happiness.

How does one go about playing this game of stacking? To play any game you must know the rules. However, just playing by the rules won't give you any advantage over your opponent. Everyone must play by the rules or get ejected from the game. A fair unfair advantage comes from knowing the rules and exploiting every loophole to your advantage. Exploiting loopholes is not cheating—it is smart. Very smart.

Investor, author, philanthropist and entrepreneur Tim Ferriss gives a great example of this tactic in his bestselling book *The 4-Hour Workweek*. In Chinese kickboxing, the way to win is to fight your way to victory, overcoming your opponent with strength and strategy. This is done through punches, kicks and various forms of attack. On a dare and with only four weeks of training, Ferriss entered the 1999 Chinese kickboxing tournament. Ferriss knew he was not a better fighter. He was new to the sport, and his opponents had been training for years. However, after studying the rules, Ferriss found a loophole.

It is considered a technical knockout if your opponent falls off the elevated platform three times. He made this his sole strategy. While Ferriss's competitors attacked with kicks, punches and jabs, he just pushed or pulled them until they fell off. His only chance to win was being a smarter fighter, not a better one. This method was considered taboo by other athletes and judges. It lacked finesse and sportsmanship and carried the stench of cheating. But to the chagrin of his naysayers, it was effective. In fact, it was so effective he became the gold medalist. The techniques he pioneered are now standard practices in the sport.

When it comes to the mind, our unconscious has a fair unfair advantage. It is vast and large and mostly unknowable to conscious awareness. It's like dark matter in the universe. Scientists believe it is there but can neither see it nor measure it. They must study it through inference of its impact on the objects around it. Stephen Hawking noted in his 2013 speech at The California Institute of Technology, "Normal matter is only 5 percent of the energy density of the known universe; 27 percent is dark matter, 68 percent is dark energy."[1] Our conscious awareness is similarly disadvantaged in regard to our unconscious. We do not have direct access to this part of our mind, but from personality to our heartbeat, these automatic systems exert profound influence on our lives.

Here are two examples of how your unconscious functions in daily life. Think of a scary moment from your childhood. Got it? Mine was when I was ten years old and nearly

---

1 http://www.redorbit.com/news/space/1112825715/dark-matter-god-topics-caltech-stephen-hawking-041813/#33WHODCMAdhUUEKZ.99

stepped on an adult water moccasin while playing in the woods with my cousin. This deadly snake bites 7,000–8,000 people a year of which about five die. Where was this memory seconds ago? It was encoded in the unconscious regions of my brain waiting for retrieval.

Here's another example. Have you ever found yourself doing or saying things that you later regretted? For example, you are at a party. It's getting late and everyone has had a few too many drinks. In his inebriated state, your boyfriend makes a joke at your expense that lands flat in the room. You feel embarrassed. Your friends give you "the look." It's an awkward moment, but it passes.

Realizing your boyfriend is intoxicated and not typically a jerk, you cut him some slack. You try to brush it off and return to saying goodbye to your friends. But you can't brush it off. You excuse yourself from the conversation to get another drink. Once you fill your glass, you make your way to the bathroom and suddenly break down in tears.

In a fit of what you later describe as temporary insanity, you burst from the bathroom and march over to your boyfriend screaming, "You have disrespected me for the last time, you jerk! It's over! Go find someone else to be your punching bag!"

You break down sobbing in the arms of your friends. Your now ex-boyfriend tries to comfort you, but you shun him. Your girlfriends come to your aid and escort you to the back porch where you apologize for ruining the party. You don't know what came over you.

What happened was there were parts of you that had been keeping a silent tally of all the rude comments your boyfriend has been making lately. His insensitivity has kept you awake at night, which in turn affected your focus at work. These parts of you were exhausted with his immaturity. They felt you deserved better, and tonight was the last straw. With the help of some liquid courage those parts pushed back. They refused to be anyone's "punching bag" any longer. This storm of temporary insanity has, in fact, been brewing in your unconscious, keeping meticulous account of his indiscretions. Tonight they had enough and burst into your consciousness with a rage they have been carrying for months.

Most of us only have a cursory understanding of our unconscious, our personality and the multi-layered structures of our mind. Yet these are pathways to gaining a fair unfair advantage, in your relationships, professional life and personal happiness. When I say fair unfair advantage I do not mean being deceptive or manipulative. I just mean knowing certain information that most other people don't know and understanding how to use that information to your benefit. This is what gives you a fair unfair advantage in the game of life.

If personality, adult attachment and parts are the games, then what are the rules? The first rule is that none of us can directly access our unconscious. It's like mental dark energy. The second rule is to learn to catch thoughts, emotions and behaviors as they emerge from your unconscious as quickly as possible. The third rule is stacking: putting one good decision on top of the other like a big pile of pancakes. Here are the steps involved in stacking.

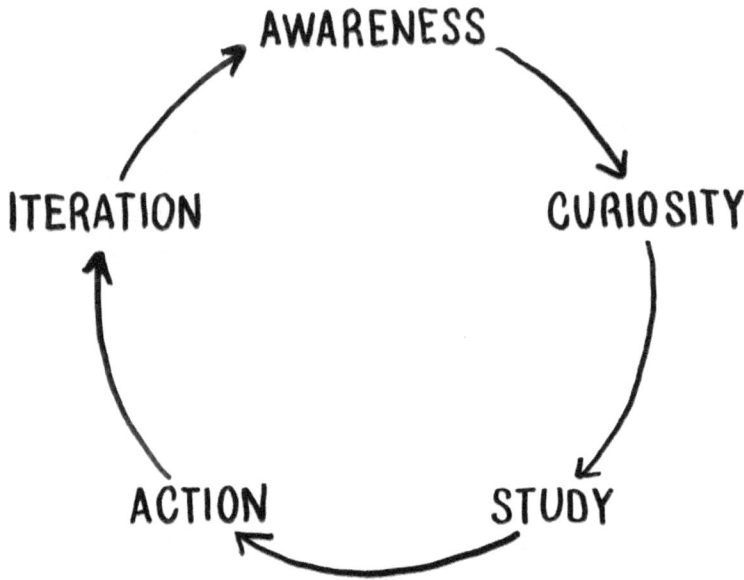

AWARENESS

Every solution to every problem you will ever have must begin with awareness. In other words, you can't solve a problem you don't know exists. Once you are aware that something isn't right, you have a choice. You can ignore it, pretend it isn't there or move toward it with curiosity.

CURIOSITY

How have other people solved a similar problem to the one you're facing? Is there a book, blog, TED Talk that you can Google? What about friends? Mentors? Professionals? Online courses? In this era of technology, there are more resources available than ever before. They won't come and find you, though. You must be curious enough to seek them out.

STUDY

Once you have found a handful of quality resources or possible solutions to your dilemma, you must create a space in your life to learn. When you become a student of life, you will bring mindfulness (not perfection) to your daily thoughts and interactions. These will be your guide, revealing what you value, what works and where to go next.

ACTION

There comes a time when action is required. Nothing will replace getting off the sidelines and into the game of life. Thinking is necessary. Planning is wise. Learning will make you a better player. However, you must put yourself in "the way of change," as John O'Donohue calls it. There is no way around the hard work of facing your fears.

ITERATION

Iteration means to pause and reflect on what you have done to see how it can be improved. Once you understand what works and what doesn't, you can refine. As someone once said, "What do you get for all your hard work? More hard work." These are the strategies that will build a resilient mind and give you a fair, unfair advantage in life, love and work.

4

STACKING – PART 2

S.T.A.R.

Louis VI first carried the oriflamme into battle in 1124[1]. In Latin oriflamme means "golden flame" *(aurea flamma)*, and historically the banner was solid red or red with orange lettering. It became the battle standard of the king of France in the Middle Ages. Originally it was not a symbol of war but a sacred banner displayed at the Abbey of St. Denis near Paris.

Its uses included striking fear in the hearts of the enemy. One method for doing this was to declare that when the oriflamme was raised, no prisoners were taken. In other words, kill everyone you see. According to legend, the red symbolized ferocity and cruelty of showing no mercy to

[1] https://en.wikipedia.org/wiki/Oriflamme

enemies. The noblemen were especially frightened of this tactic as it was customary for royalty to be taken alive in battle. Once the skirmish was settled, a ransom would be paid for their safe return.

In modern times, oriflamme has evolved to represent a symbol, insignia or ideal that inspires loyalty and courage. While most of us will never march into battle with a banner, we still enter battles with ourselves, our circumstances, our past, our present and our future every day. As you work through each level of greater self-awareness, the message is clear to anyone or anything opposing your progress: take no prisoners. You are out to win. You want to succeed. You want to thrive. You want everyone you love to thrive in their lives as well.

The irony is that, unlike battle, you are your worst enemy and your greatest hero. You have within yourself every authority to build an empire or lay ruins to your life. Hour after hour, weary soldiers file into my office for refuge from the war they are waging. They want to be trained in the ways of the wise and courageous warrior.

What these warriors want is for someone to tell them something they haven't heard and can't Google. They want their worldview questioned. They want their beliefs challenged because something isn't working. They believe their impossible problems have solutions, and they can be truly happy. They are desperate to understand why they do what they do and what they can change.

Below is a tool that can offer clear insight and deep wisdom. It will infuse you with courage. It is called your S.T.A.R.

diagram, and it includes your Enneagram type and Style of Rejuvenation (Introversion/Amibversion/Extroversion), Attachment Style, Instinctual Layers (Sexual/Social/Self-Preservation) plus Self Energy. Here is an example:

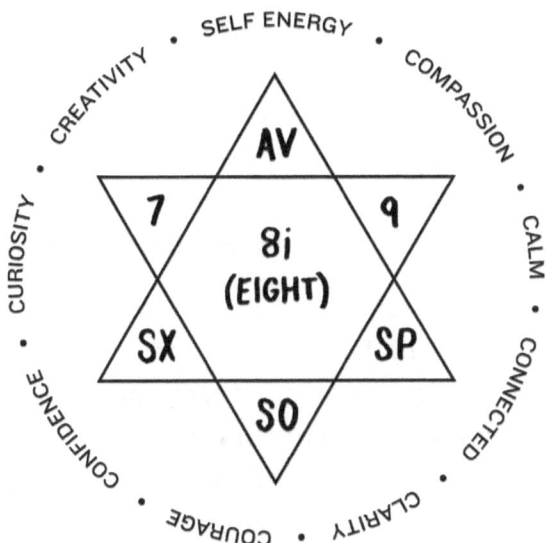

Kevin Kelly, cofounder of *Wired* magazine, describes technology as any inanimate creation by man. Included in this description are spoons, pianos and computers. Using Kelly's definition, this S.T.A.R. is a "technology" that illuminates your temperament. In other words, this is *temperament technology*.

The most perplexing issue with technology—and maybe our saving grace—is that technology, as we know it today, is inanimate. It cannot think for itself. A book cannot read itself, but if it could it would have consciousness. If the long history of life on earth reveals anything it is that beings who possess *consciousness* will eventually create two forms of awareness: conscious and unconscious.

Just as the veil between life and death has yet to be pierced, there is an impenetrable cloak between our waking conscious and our vast, hidden unconscious. The mystery of our unconscious is only revealed through conscious thoughts and actions. If we choose to ignore the symbolism in our behaviors (e.g., excessive drinking, road rage or dating the same type of incompatible person), we are missing the only opportunities we have to rewrite the internal code causing these malignant, self-destructive patterns.

Our unconscious can only speak in symbols. There is a dance that happens between our hidden mind and our sentient mind. The hidden mind sees a problem and needs to send a message. The sentient mind must translate the secret code. However, the sentient mind can only use the tools it has developed to translate the message. If it doesn't have the proper tools (i.e., maturity, wisdom, experience, knowledge), then the message fades away, and an opportunity to learn something new or head off a disaster is missed.

The S.T.A.R. is a hexagonal tool where each element is an in-depth method for understanding unconscious motivations. The S.T.A.R. diagram has twenty variables that include:

- **Primary Enneagram Type:** 1–9

- **Enneagram Instincts:** Sexual (One-To-One Bonding) / Social / Self-Preservation)

- **Enneagram Wings:** The two numbers on each side of the primary

- **Enneagram Number**

- **Style of Rejuvenation:** Introversion / Extroversion / Ambiversion

- **Adult Attachment Styles:** Secure / Anxious / Avoidant

Of these twenty variables, only eight are used for each diagram. This results in 125,970 possible permutations. In other words, every person you know (mother, brother, friend, boss) has one of nearly 126,000 ways of being innately configured. And this is just using three psychological models. There are dozens of unique, scientifically validated methods of explaining temperament. We are complex creatures who need sophisticated tools to understand ourselves and each other.

At the end of this book there is a blank S.T.A.R. diagram for you to inscribe with your own personal information you will learn throughout this book. Below is a brief example of each layer and the symbolism embedded within.

The borders encompassing the diagram symbolize the qualities of your *True Self* expressed through *Self Energy*. Your *True Self* is intended to be the leader, and this is done through *Self Energy*. This is the reason for *Self Energy* being located at the apex of the diagram.

The six-pointed star holds enough information for anyone to live a mindful, joyful, happy life full of gratitude and courage.

Here is an explanation of the example above. It will give you a brief overview of each dynamic element:

1. **8i** – This represents both the primary Enneagram type and identifies your style of rejuvenation. The three styles are introvert, extrovert or a balance between the two called an ambivert. In this example, this person is a **Type 8 - Challenger** and is **Introverted**. The number is writ large and in bold to symbolize the primacy of personality in our daily lives. More than any other attribute, your personality will dictate how you filter your daily interactions.

2. The **"AV"** at the top of the hexagram represents this person's Adult Attachment style. The three options are avoidant (AV), anxious (AX) and secure (S).

3. **Type 9 & Type 7** – These represent the Wings of the **Type 8,** which influence the primary personality. Given that the Enneagram is illustrated in a circle, each number has two numbers on each side. These are considered the Wings of each type. For example, a **Type 8** may move into their **Type 9** Wing when at work, which would manifest in their being more laid back and easygoing. Whereas the **Type 8** might become like a more relaxed **Type 7** after a few drinks with friends.

4. **SP, SX & SO** – These represent the instincts of *self-preservation, sexual (one-to-one bonding)* and *social*. For this example, this person's primary instinct is *Self Preservation*, which is represented by its placement on the lower left section. The secondary instinct is *Sexual (One-to-One Bonding)*, represented by being placed in

the lower right section. The least developed instinct of *Social* is represented by sitting at the bottom of the S.T.A.R. Just as each person is influenced by both of their Wings, each person has all three instincts. What makes one more dominant than another is how an individual has learned to successfully navigate relationships. When a certain instinct works for an individual, they tend to rely more heavily on that instinct while relying less on the others.

5. **Self-Energy** – The majority of this book is dedicated to understanding the 8 C's of Self-Energy. These eight words surrounding the S.T.A.R. symbolically represent what is needed for personal growth and advancement in life.

5
—

THE CYCLE OF SELF-DETERMINATION

In case this point is not abundantly clear so far, let me repeat it: Every solution to every problem you will ever have must begin with awareness. The reason is simple. You cannot change what you have not named. But if solving impossible problems were as easy as raising awareness, there would be many more people in the *Self Actualized* level of Maslow's Hierarchy of Needs.

For some it takes a lifetime before understanding the root causes of their impossible problems. Others never manage more than a faint hint of understanding. These unlucky folks were often given too few tools and too many obstacles at too young an age.

Many of the stories throughout this book are about making the right choice at the wrong time. Awareness comes but it's too late. How many repentant murderers are on death row?[1] How many divorcees wished they had their first marriage back? How many alcoholics wished they had not driven drunk *after* the accident?

Awareness alone is not enough. Nashville is awash in "coulda been a contenda" stories of failed entertainment careers. You can't swing a vintage Martin D-45 in this town without hitting one incredible musician after another. Many potential stars with exceptional talent wash out because they were ill-equipped to beat their addiction or any number of other demons. As a result, they checked out of the game too early. They never did the hard work to make themselves truly happy in the Aristotelian sense.

The *Cycle of Self-Determination* offers insight into the way the unconscious maneuvers back and forth between healthy and unhealthy responses to life. Our everyday problems are a dime a dozen. Easy come. Easy go. But the impossible problems, the ones that stick around for years and kick you in the face before your feet even hit the floor in the morning, are rooted in the unconscious realm. If the unconscious is the domain of impossible problems, then the best chance for success is to meet them there.

This vast unconscious network consumes gigabytes of information every second. Its primary function is to analyze and process this data through a series of internal filters such as personality, attachment style and parts

---

[1] https://www.tdcj.state.tx.us/death_row/dr_executed_offenders.html

Once conclusions are drawn and adequate solutions vetted, they are integrated into the conscious mind for action. Other activities for which the unconscious is responsible are automatic operations such as heartbeat, digestion, memory storage, etc.

$$\text{PARTS} \left\{ \text{O} \right\} \left\{ \begin{array}{l} \triangle \text{ — ATTACHMENT} \\ \square \text{ — PERSONALITY} \end{array} \right.$$

UNCONSCIOUS

Most of the decisions we make fall into the category of *Automatic Reactions*. Many of these behaviors initially took a lot of effort to learn but now run on autopilot. They streamline life by minimizing the thoughtfulness needed to complete the action. Think how cumbersome it would be if you had to pause and have a conscious thought every time you threw a ball or washed your hands (e.g., lift my right hand, move forward, turn the silver knob, etc.).

AUTOMATIC REACTIONS

$$\text{PARTS} \left\{ \text{O} \right\} \left\{ \begin{array}{l} \triangle \text{ — ATTACHMENT} \\ \square \text{ — PERSONALITY} \end{array} \right.$$

UNCONSCIOUS

For the most part, the results of our *Automatic Reactions* are beneficial. Our daily work is an example of how this "automation" is helpful. When these *Automatic Reactions* work smoothly, our unconscious sends the message that *Life Is Good*. This means each step in the process worked as predicted, confirming our preconceived ideas. This information is stored away for future reference so when the same or similar events occur we instinctively know how to respond. Our rewards are quick solutions to problems and a life that flows smoothly.

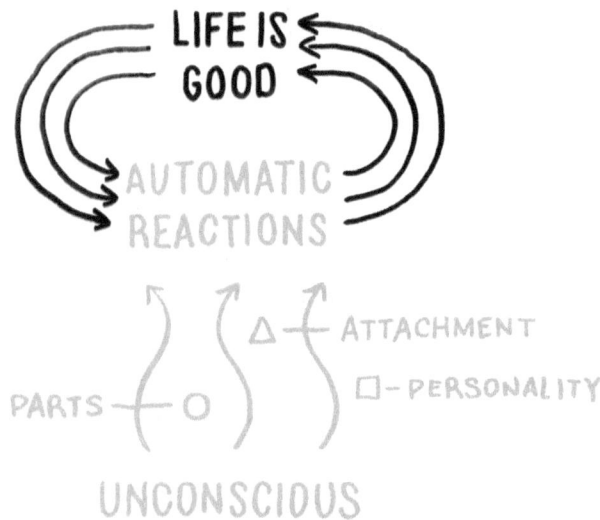

But what do you do when the warning lights start sounding on the control panel of your brain, signaling a problem? This intuitive warning creates a tension telling us *Something Isn't Right*, which results in a *Pain Point* or *Suffering*. Often this *Suffering* is a pregnant unknowing heralding the coming labor pains of some yet-to-be defined problem or challenge. It is difficult to sense something is wrong yet be unable to identify the source. We can handle most of what life throws our way. We are resilient if nothing else. However, to be in the limbo state of not knowing is an agony all its own.

As we grow curious about our *Suffering* (as opposed to ignoring or suppressing it), it inevitably leads to greater and greater *Awareness*. As I have said before and I will say many times again—the solution to any problem you will ever have must start with awareness. This *Awareness* may start out as a very dim understanding like the lights on a high school baseball field that must first warm up before reaching full brightness.

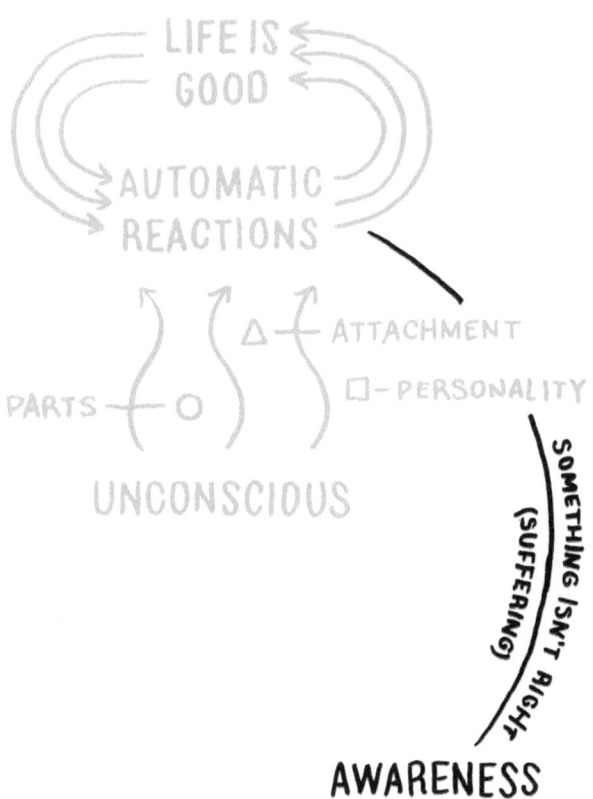

Once you become aware of the problem, then you begin to *Want Something Different*. You want a solution. You want to mend the relationship with your parents. You want to get another job. You want to move to a city you have always dreamt of living. You know you need to break up with your girlfriend because it isn't healthy for either of you. However, this new dawning awareness circles back around to...you guessed it—*Suffering*. You suffer because you want what you do not have, and you do not yet know if you will be able to get what you want.

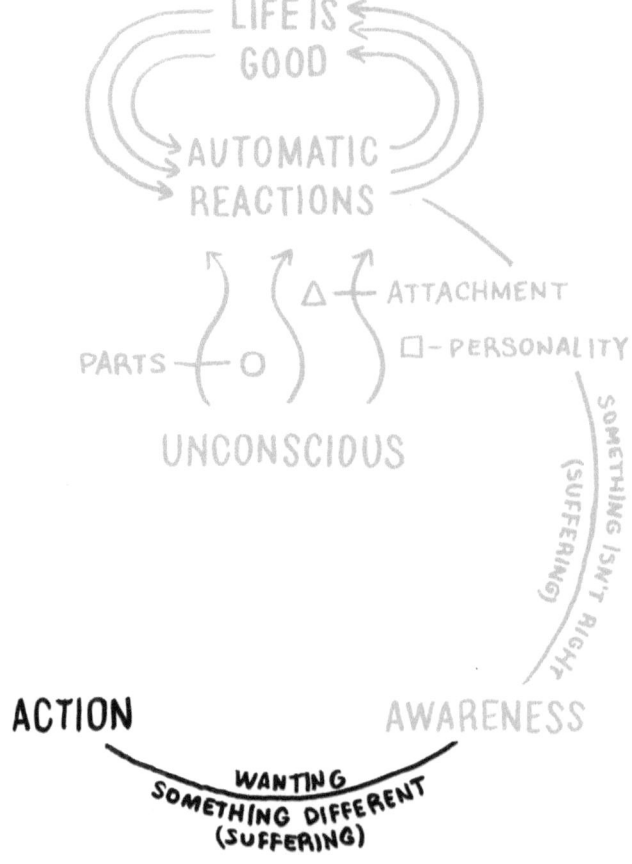

THE CYCLE OF SELF-DETERMINATION

At any point in this process you have the choice to cut and run and return to your old *Automatic Reactions* (yeah, the ones that caused these problems in the first place). This could mean you choose not to break up with your girlfriend. You know it will cause her pain, and she has threatened to kill herself if you end it. This could mean you withdraw emotionally back into your protective shell when you are around your parents instead of trying to build a bridge or confront them with the ways you feel they failed you. It could mean staying in your current job because finding a new job and moving to a new city is just too much work. These are the *Automatic Reactions* we mindlessly repeat. The problem with this strategy is that if you ignore your problems, they don't go away; they bypass the *Life Is Good* loop and careen headlong back into the familiar *Something's Not Right* cycle.

If you succeed in gaining *Awareness* that *Something Isn't Right* and you realize you *Want Something Different*, the next step is to take action and *Do Something Different*. Here again you have many choices to make. There are many areas of life that require your attention on a regular basis, from your finances to your health to your relationships. If you fail to act differently in any of these areas, you go back into the *Automatic Reaction* cycle and repeat the process from the start. Here is where significant damage is done to your psyche. When you fail to act differently, you repeat your *Negative Loop* by *Doing The Same Thing*.

In this familiar loop, you avoid dealing with your problems and exile your fear and pain as far away from consciousness as possible. The problems still exist, but they might as well be in another galaxy. Just because you no longer feel the discomfort of your problems doesn't mean they no longer exist. They have simply descended to the unconscious realm. Here they clandestinely influence both your body and brain. This unhealthy way of dealing with problems creates anxiety, depression, despair and hopelessness. This swirl of negativity can easily lead to countless addictions and, in extreme cases, suicidal ideation.

One of the greatest tragedies in this loop are the lost opportunities you were never aware of that could have changed the direction of your life. When you ignore or repress these and other symptoms, you are overlooking the very clues that could lead you out of the dark forest of confusion. When you ignore your loneliness and say no to a trip with friends, there is no way of knowing what you missed. When you do not end unhealthy relationships, you take yourself out of the dating pool and miss meeting new people who may be better suited to meet your needs. You simply cannot know what you do not know.

THE CYCLE OF SELF-DETERMINATION

If you find the courage to take action and *Do Something Different*, it sends you directly into more *Suffering*. You may be noticing a pattern emerging that whatever route you take will lead you back to *Suffering*. The Buddha was right. It does not matter if you are wealthy or living paycheck to paycheck, famous or unknown, beautiful or homely—life is suffering. But not all *Suffering* is equal. Mindless, unnecessary suffering that we endure out of our fear or ignorance is painful. It seems pointless and leads to despair and hopelessness. But mindful intentional *Suffering* has a noble purpose. *Sacred Suffering* is the obstacle by which our character is strengthened and forward progress in our lives achieved. Our *Sacred Suffering* is the path that will lead us to the destination we so desperately seek.

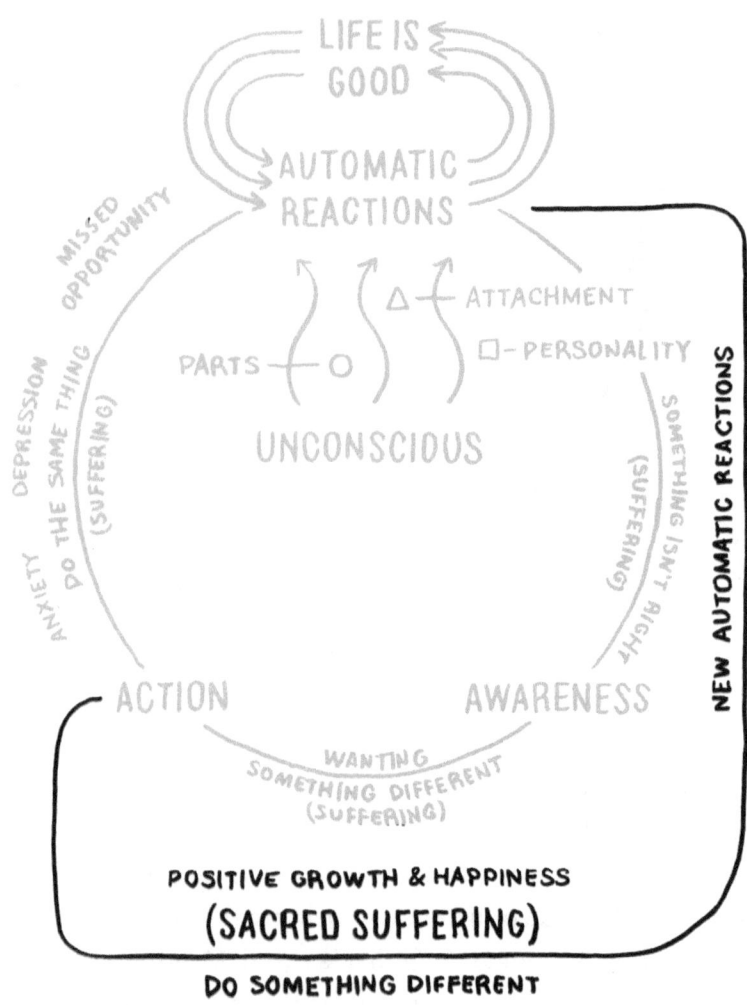

As we learn to suffer well, what we find is growth and happiness. This is Aristotle's *Good Life*. In the *Good Life*, we are soul searching. Through the affliction of difficulties we discover new, fascinating parts of our selves. We break through old limitations and tap into new potential we didn't realize we possessed. Life's tragedies become our training, preparing us for the next obstacle. Our reward for all the hard work we are doing to achieve lasting happiness is more hard work, but it is hard work with a purpose.

Often we are tasked with exerting intentional action in many areas of life all at once. We are constantly bombarded with demands from twelve primary domains of life: *marriage, parenting, profession, finances, family, sexuality, addiction, spirituality, mental health, physical health, friendship/community and healthy boundaries*. If we are struggling professionally, it will inevitably have some impact on our marriage, which will affect our physical and mental health. The last thing we feel like doing when depressed and anxious about possibly filing bankruptcy is having sex. There is a cascade effect that works both ways. That is why it is critically important to maintain our mental health with the same regularity as we maintain our dental care. One healthy decision after another is *stacking*. One unhealthy decision after another is *drifting*. This universal law was distilled with great eloquence and simplicity by Steven Gaskin, the founder of The Farm commune in Summertown, Tennessee, when he taught, "Whatever you focus on will prosper."

As you *Do Something Different* by successfully avoiding old patterns and unproductive mistakes, your system gets a much-needed boost. It is true that your efforts of challenging old habits will require you to suffer, but the great reward for *Sacred Suffering* is *Positive Growth* and *Happiness*. As you make better decisions rooted in the present, not the past, you create *New Automatic Reactions* that are healthy and constructive.

Before you know it, you are once again enjoying your relationships, satisfied with your work and developing creative, fun ways of coping with stress. You are invigorated by life not burned out. You are facing your fears. This new life, is exciting. It is filled with anticipation of what is around the next corner (a proposition that previously caused dread). By regaining control of your life, your heart, mind and soul, you are imbued with confidence, compassion, courage, clarity, connectedness, creativity, calmness and curiosity.

6

THE FOOTSTOOL & THE CLOCKTOWER

It is important for new clients to understand the therapeutic framework of the therapist. These include the beliefs about how the brain functions, how the mind works and how people heal from trauma and live happy lives. In the initial session with new clients, I share with them three models I have come to depend on after more than fifteen years as a psychotherapist. I filter all my moment-to-moment assessments and clinical decisions through these guiding principles. This triad examines the complex thoughts and actions of an individual and offers them a framework through which they can better understand why they do what they do. As they gain greater awareness, they can take thoughtful steps to change their life for the better.

It is incredible to think that the entirety of a person's life experiences are filtered through one, single organ—the brain. As we begin to decipher the mysteries of personality, attachment and parts, we gain a tremendous advantage. This advantage helps us maneuver through our blind spots. Like a ship in a storm off a rocky coast, we are less likely to crash on the rocky shores of life if we see the dangers in advance.

To simplify this explanation for clients, I draw a crude picture of a footstool on my yellow legal pad and hold it up for them to see.

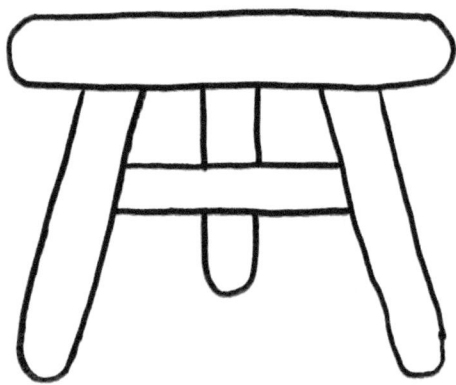

I paint a picture with broad strokes, outlining each psychological framework:

- The first leg represents the Enneagram personality system

- The second leg represents Adult Attachment
- The third leg represents Internal Family System (IFS)
- The braces connecting the legs represent mindfulness and gratitude
- The top of the stool where one would sit or stand represents spirituality

To a lesser or greater degree, we are all ruled by our unconscious. Most of us never think about our personality in a given situation, we just automatically respond. However, just because we don't think about what goes on in our unconscious doesn't mean we can't.

These three systems (Enneagram/Attachment/IFS) are part of the operating system of your unconscious. They are hardwired biologically into your DNA and influenced by the circumstances of your life. They are present with you this very moment translating, adapting and adjusting to your environment. Right now these and many other internal systems are working away solving problems and keeping you alive without you even being aware. That is both their beauty and their fatal flaw. They cannot be directly accessed by the conscious mind. Your conscious awareness must wait until a thought, feeling or sensation rises from the deep before it can respond.

Your subconscious is like your refrigerator. Yes, the one at home that's keeping your beer cold. Whether you are at work in a meeting or at home staring into its empty abyss, it's still humming away doing its job. It is the same with your unconscious. It continues to work all day every day.

I use the analogy of a footstool with clients because it is easy for me to draw and easy for clients to understand. But the reality is that the inner workings of our minds are more analogous to Big Ben, the clocktower in London, England, than a simple footstool.

The clock stands three hundred sixteen feet tall. On the outside is its enormous face for tourists to admire and locals to check the time. However, behind the ornamental façade are highly complex mechanisms. These gears and pulleys work in unison to keep the big hand in sync with the little hand and the bells chiming at just the right moment.

These systems are so finely tuned that when the time of the massive timepiece gets out of sync with Greenwich Mean Time (GMT), all the clock keeper must do to bring the time back into alignment is place a single penny or two on either side of the enormous thirteen-foot pendulum. Not surprisingly your collection of internal subconscious systems, while vast and powerful like Big Ben, are also highly sensitive to slight changes in mood, biology, health, circumstances, news, the environment and countless other variables, some of which are in your control and some not.

Just as tourists cannot see the internal mechanisms of Big Ben neither can you or anyone else see your own unconscious systems at work...that is until you expend a little effort to pay attention to them. Once you are aware of your unique personality that falls broadly into the nine categories of the Enneagram, you can see how you are programmed by your biology to act and react in particular ways. While you cannot change your internal programming, you can predict with great accuracy your response to circumstances.

For example, someone with a Type 2 Enneagram personality will automatically put other people's needs before their own. This selflessness is their greatest gift to the world. However, without insight and maturity, this becomes a great burden leading to burnout and bitterness. As this type of individual matures, when they feel the familiar tug to help someone they first check in with themselves. They ask if they *want* to give away their time and energy in this moment. This self-preservation helps them maintain a healthy groundedness. They adapt to their greatest gift without letting it overwhelm them. This allows them to give out of their abundance rather than feeling constantly drained and overextended.

The same is true for your attachment system. Once you become aware that you inevitably attach to others in a predictable yet unconscious way, you can begin to exert influence and dictate what you need to feel secure in the relationship. If the other person cannot meet your needs, this doesn't mean they are a bad person. Neither does it mean you need to spend your precious time and energy trying to convince them to act in ways they do not want or are not able to act. This will save both of you time and unnecessary suffering.

Finally, once you begin to see your inner world is a kaleidoscope of "parts," you can then take care of each part's individual needs. You won't see the erratic and often conflicting conversations you have with yourself as madness but an active and vibrant community of personalities where each is vying for your best interests.

The ultimate goal is to create permanent, healthy habits through a deeper understanding of ourselves that prevents many problems from ever occurring. We want resilient strategies that are agile and can adapt quickly to the rapid pace of modern life and relationships. We want the quiet confidence that comes with knowing we have the wisdom, compassion and perseverance to overcome, regardless of what comes our way.

7
—

ENNEAGRAM

Physicist Leonard Mlodinow writes in his book *Subliminal: How Your Unconscious Mind Rules Your Behavior*, "If you really want to understand yourself and others, and, beyond that, if you really want to overcome many of the obstacles that prevent you from living your fullest, richest life, you need to understand the influence of the subliminal world that is hidden within each of us." Understanding how your unconscious works and how you can manipulate it for your benefit is a sure path to happiness. Let's begin this journey into the unconscious realms with personality.

Imagine yourself a young teenage boy who lived a thousand years ago. You are part of a medium-sized tribe of nearly one thousand people. Your father is a skilled hunter and tanner. Your mother weaves baskets, tools and clothing from the hides of the animals he kills. As for you, you are tall and strong—a good head and shoulders above the other children your age. You are liked by your peers and have a calm but confident disposition, even for your young age. You rarely squabble with your four brothers and three sisters.

One day the chief of the tribe comes to visit your wigwam. Your parents invite him in, and you notice they are honored yet frightened. They understand his power as they have seen him deal fairly but harshly with wayward members. As is the tradition with these types of meetings, you and all of your brothers and sisters sit around the chief as the parents make his meal. Once the chief and all the children are served, the parents take their place standing behind their children. Everyone knows the chief is evaluating each child for future roles in the tribe.

The chief begins by asking the youngest children what they most enjoy eating and which games they like playing. Next he asks the parents if they are having trouble with any of the children and if any of the children are sick. Your father speaks plainly and honestly with the chief, knowing false or misleading statements are not tolerated.

Suddenly the chief turns to you and says, "I need your help settling a dispute." You are frightened by the sudden, unexpected attention but hide your fear. "Anything you ask, Chief."

"As you know there were two friends arguing over a girl that resulted in a fight. The one young man struck the other with a stone hammer. As a result he may die soon.

What do you think the punishment for the young man who struck his friend should be?"

Your parents stiffen, and you see they are anxious to hear your response. You heard rumors of the incident the day before and were very sad to hear about the tragedy. You were not close friends of either as they were older than you.

"Chief," you respond quickly, "the penalty in our tribe for murder is death unless for reasons of self-defense. However, since he is not dead yet, any decision about the offender's fate should be put off until the fate of the other young man is known. Also, we should not forget that there are not two but three families that are grieving here: the two boys' families and the young girl who may feel partially responsible. We must make it a priority to care for them as this terrible situation may result in a great disturbance in our tribe and create enemies where enemies did not exist before. Finally," you end your comments to the chief, "I do not have enough information to make a reasonable judgment on what should or should not be done. I know you are a fair and just leader. I also know that you have very difficult decisions to make. Sometimes there are no good options."

When you finish talking, you look to your parents for approval or disapproval. Your mother is smiling. Your father gives you a nod of confidence.

The chief stares at you for several long beats, not giving anything away about how he feels about your response. He takes a deep breath, and you feel your feet and hands go numb.

"You are correct that you do not have enough information to make a wise decision. Come take a walk with me after this meal, and I will discuss this issue with you further." The chief picks up his bowl and begins eating. This signals the end of the discussion. Everyone in the family follows suit.

Later, after the sun has set and the rest of the family is asleep, you and your father sit in silence around the fire. You both know you are being groomed to be the next chief of the tribe. How does the chief come to his conclusions about on whom to bestow his blessing?

This chief and many others like him had some form of what today we call "personality assessment tools" to make good personnel decisions. Corporations use a battery of psychological assessments to determine who is good for what position. However, a thousand years ago, tribes didn't have human resource departments to catalogue each member of the tribe and their unique skills and talents. Much of the heavy lifting of decision-making was on the leader or small council. Imagine if there were a system passed down from generation to generation of how to understand who would make a good warrior, priest, chef, architect and woodworker. Wouldn't this be invaluable for leaders?

―

The precise origins of the Enneagram are unknown. However, there are some tantalizing clues as to its history, as well as a solid foundation for its more recent past.

The two oldest existing texts in Western literature are *The Iliad* and *The Odyssey*. *The Odyssey* chronicles Odysseus's journey home where during his travels he visits nine islands that align with the nine archetypes of the Enneagram.[1] It may have been through his association with the Chaldeans and Persians that Homer gained knowledge of the Enneagram. As with modern-day seekers, Odysseus's epic journey is an allegory for our return home to our *True Self*.

Due to the uniformity and complexity of the Enneagram symbol, some have posited that its origins can be traced to the sacred geometric "seal" of Pythagoras as well as the mystical mathematics of the Platonists. They used a symbol similar to the Enneagram to illustrate special qualities and relationships between numbers.

Throughout history there have been philosophical and cosmological teachings focused on nine types, including philosopher and mystic Plotinus referring to the nine human virtues in his seminal work *The Enneads*. Imbedded in the Jewish mystical tradition Kabbalah is a creation story whereby the universe was created out of the ten aspects of God. However, God wanted to see his own creation and withdrew into his own being, leaving nine aspects of God to create the world. In the Sufi tradition, there exist symbols similar to the Enneagram. Specifically the Naqshbandi Aliya teachings of The Levels of the Heart and The 9 Lataif, which includes the 9 States of Humanity.

---

1 https://en.wikipedia.org/wiki/Geography_of_the_Odyssey

In Christianity, Franciscan mystic Ramon Llull spent nine years in solitude before teaching a nine-principled philosophy attempting to reconcile various faith traditions with each other. Jesuit mathematician Athanasius Kircher created a symbol for a 17th century text that is similar in design to the Enneagram.

While these philosophies and theologies are man's attempts to understand himself and God, the true source of how the Enneagram came into being is shrouded in mystery. What is known is that Russian mystic and teacher George Gurdjieff possibly first learned of the Enneagram in an Afghan monastery, though there are very few facts to base the origins prior to this event.

In the 1960s, Oscar Ichazo taught something he called Protoanalysis, of which the Enneagram played a prominent part. Through Ichazo, Claudio Naranjo, a Chilean psychiatrist, learned of the Enneagram and began teaching it himself. He passed the tradition along to Jesuit Bob Ochs who introduced the concept to Christian communities in the United States. Among them were Don Riso and Russ Hudson. They later founded *The Enneagram Institute*.

Here is the Enneagram symbol with its nine types:

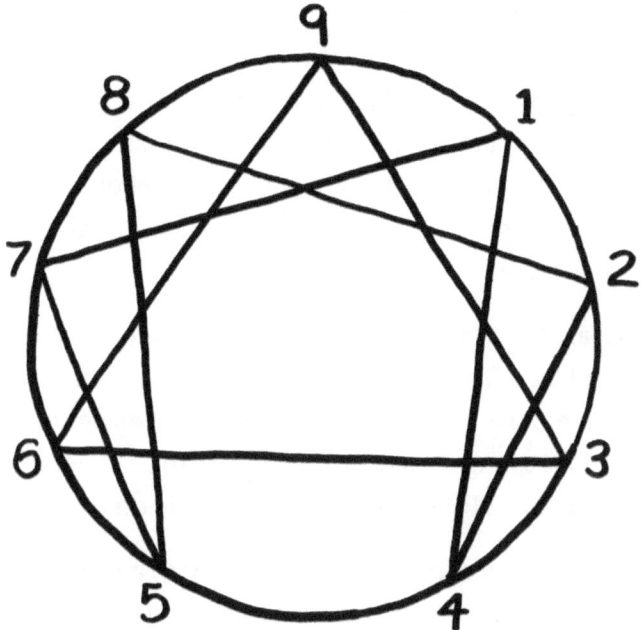

One caveat regarding typing yourself or others is that you cannot easily guess a person's type simply by their actions. Two people might do the same thing for different reasons. When someone first learns of the Enneagram and "gets it," they are filled with excitement and want to share it with others. They often make the mistake of typing others too quickly or inaccurately. It is not uncommon for those new to the Enneagram to use it in ways that are manipulative or judgmental. Additionally, there are those who attempt to label public figures based solely on behavior. What you cannot know by a person's actions alone is their motivation.

Here is a description of two different types. A Type One is known for doing the right thing and making sure others do the right thing as well. This can often come across as judgmental and harsh, when in fact they are simply trying to abide by the rules. A Type Two, on the other hand, cares deeply about other people, fosters relationships and takes care of others' needs. They are the type of people who will stay after the party to help the host clean up after everyone else is gone.

Here is an example of two types engaging in the same behavior but with different motivations. Type One comes across an elderly lady with a walker at a stoplight. Seeing that she is moving slowly he asks if he can help her and she heartily agrees. He walks her across and is on his way.

A Type Two comes upon an elderly lady at a stoplight and compliments her on her hair and the fancy streamers coming off of her walker. The elderly lady comments that her grandchildren put them on there for her, and she loves them. The light changes, signaling for everyone to walk across. The Type Two takes the elderly lady's arm and helps her across the street. Once across she hugs the elderly woman and wishes her a wonderful day.

Both Type One and Type Two helped the elderly lady across the street. What is the difference? The Type One helped the elderly lady because his essential energy tells him it is the right thing to do. The Type Two helps the elderly lady across the street because she cares for her well-being and has compassion for her. That is the essential energy of a Type Two—Two very different energies indeed.

A person's essential energy is expressed through both words and what they choose to do and choose not to do. Here is a list of each type's essential energy:

Type One
I must be perfect, make the right decision and do the right thing. I must make sure everyone else does the same.

Type Two
I must take care of you. Often I will put your needs before mine.

Type Three
I must succeed and be seen as successful.

Type Four
I must be unique and be seen as unique.

Type Five
I must think before I act...sometimes this takes a long time.

Type Six
I must be loyal to friends, family and causes. I must be safe.

Type Seven
I must experience life to its fullest.

Type Eight
I must be strong above all.

Type Nine
I must be at peace with myself and others.

There are many excellent tests online to determine your type, or go to rebbuxton.com/enneagram for more information.

The layers of the Enneagram are multitudinous. For example, The Enneagram Institute teaches many facets of the Enneagram beyond the primary type. Here are a few examples: the centers of the head (5,6,7), heart (2, 3, 4) and body (8, 9, 1); the direction of integration and disintegration; wings, levels of developments and harmonics, to name just a few.

Beatrice Chestnut talks about three basic instincts of the Enneagram known as social, sexual (one-to-one bonding) and self-preservation in her book *The Complete Enneagram: 27 Paths to Greater Self-Knowledge*:

> Grouped according to their centers, the personality types and the connecting lines between them draw the figure of the ancient mystical symbol that is the Enneagram diagram. Beyond the three centers and the nine types is a third level of depth that divides each of the nine Enneagram types into three distinct sub-personalities, or "subtypes," based on the relative emphasis of three basic instincts. The resulting twenty-seven subtypes are unique personality types based on how each of the nine types are shaped by the three most central instinctual drives that we all share.

These three basic instincts are arranged in order from primary, secondary and blind spot. These basic instincts have such a pull on a person's primary Enneagram type that given the order of a person's instincts in conjunction with a person's type creates not nine but twenty-seven unique personalities.

To explore what these instincts look like in the wild, let's use a simple example of three friends at a party.

The first friend's primary instinct is *sexual/one-to-one bonding*. When she arrives at the party, she slowly mingles, getting a glass of wine and taking in the crowd. She may chat with friends or even strangers, but she is more interested in having a personal connection with one other person or maybe a very small group. Once she finds this person or persons, she will most likely spend the majority of the evening in this conversation. She thrives on the energy created by deep connection to another person. This connection could be someone she knows well or a stranger.

The second friend has a high *self-preservation* instinct. He is on guard as soon as he walks in the door. Unlike his *one-to-one* friend, his initial instinct, which he is most likely not even aware of, is scanning for situations that make him feel safe (e.g., friends he knows) and watching out for threats (e.g., obnoxious drunk guy). Outwardly he is calm and inwardly he may feel relaxed, but he never stops scanning for potential danger. If anyone starts to get out of hand at the party, he will be one of the first to notice. This friend will most likely be the first to want to leave.

The third friend has a high *social* instinct. She may be the life of the party or a social butterfly that flits about the room saying hello and making everyone feel welcome. She wants to connect with as many people as possible at the party and therefore cannot get too bogged down in a long conversation with one person. This is the friend who will want to go to the after-party and drags her other *self-preservation* and *sexual* friends along with her.

What type describes you best in social situations? Are you the one who finds someone interesting and dives deep into conversation? Are you the one who is vigilant and attentive? Are you the social butterfly, meeting people and making connections? Visit rebbuxton.com/instincts for a full description of each instinct. Once you know your Enneagram type, wings and instinctual order return to the s.t.a.r. diagram at the back of the book and enter your Enneagram and instinctual stack results.

8

ATTACHMENT

John Bowlby is the father of attachment theory. His study of the relationship between adolescent delinquent behaviors and how those behaviors related to separation from their primary caregivers was the basis for this field of study. Bowlby's student and later colleague Mary Ainsworth was responsible for testing Bowlby's ideas. She played a primary role in suggesting there were several different attachment styles. Her systematic studying of the parent-child bond sparked a deeper understanding of the individual differences in how people attach to one another. Ainsworth created something called the Strange Situation Test. R. Chris Frayley writes in his research paper, *A Brief Overview of Adult Attachment Theory and Research*:

> In the strange situation, 12-month-old infants and their parents are brought to the laboratory and,

systematically, separated from and reunited with one another. In the strange situation, most children (i.e., about 60%) behave in the way implied by Bowlby's "normative" theory. They become upset when the parent leaves the room, but, when he or she returns, they actively seek the parent and are easily comforted by him or her. Children who exhibit this pattern of behavior are often called SECURE.

Other children (about 20% or less) are ill-at-ease initially, and, upon separation, become extremely distressed. Importantly, when reunited with their parents, these children have a difficult time being soothed, and often exhibit conflicting behaviors that suggest they want to be comforted, but that they also want to "punish" the parent for leaving. These children are often called ANXIOUS.

The third pattern of attachment that Ainsworth and her colleagues documented is called AVOIDANT. Avoidant children (about 20%) don't appear too distressed by the separation, and, upon reunion, actively avoid seeking contact with their parent, sometimes turning their attention to play objects on the laboratory floor.

One point to note about AVOIDANTLY attached children in the study: Sensors were attached to measure heart rate and other biometric data. The interesting discovery was that while outwardly the AVOIDANT child did not appear to be showing symptoms of anxiety when separated, internally they were having the same biological stress responses as the ANXIOUSLY attached children *but weren't showing it.*

This is an important finding as it substantiates the idea that while ANXIOUSLY attached individuals protest and perseverate on relationships, AVOIDANTLY attached individuals suppress their true feelings. This disconnection between feeling and behavior creates a dissonance that often leaves the partners of AVOIDANTLY attached individuals in the dark about what is happening and why.

Following are descriptions of three primary types of adult attachment. As noted previously those three types are: secure, anxious and avoidant. When reading each paragraph, think about how your current or past partners would describe you in the relationship. How would your mother and father describe you as a child? How would your friends rate your level of availability to them and your willingness to engage in personal, meaningful conversations?

After reading each attachment style below, return to your S.T.A.R. diagram to fill in your results.

ANXIOUS

You are known for being very close with your romantic partners physically and emotionally. However, often your partners will find your behavior "clingy" or "needy." One of your fears is that your partner does not want to be as close to you as you want to be to them. Due to this uncertainty about your relationship, you spend a lot of time and emotional energy thinking about ways to head off potential problems. You are so tuned in to your relationships you sometimes tend to be highly sensitive to your partner's moods or behaviors.

For example, if your partner does not text you back after a relatively short period of time, you might begin to worry if something is wrong or what you may have done to upset them. This ruminating behavior may cause you to bombard them with further texts demanding, "Where are you? What are you doing? Who are you with?"

These types of behaviors tend to push people away (especially avoidantly attached partners) when what you intend is to draw them closer. When someone shows you ongoing attention and respects your need for closeness, you begin to relax and not worry so much about the state of the relationship. This type of anxious behavior is not limited to romantic partnerships. It will manifest in friend and family relationships as well.

AVOIDANT

Your independence is your main priority whether it is a friendship, romantic relationship or professional affiliation. You desire to be close to others, but being too close too often makes you uncomfortable. When you feel too much pressure for intimacy (physical or emotional), you often react by pushing others away. In romantic relationships you don't spend much time worrying about the relationship or being rejected. However, you are not a robot and desire deep connection with those you care about. The difficulty comes when you do not express your feelings in the moment when you feel the need to withdraw from others for your own benefit. This secret desire creates confusion with those closest to you as they wonder if they have done something to cause you to want to pull away. As a result, your partners often complain about you being emotionally distant.

SECURE

Deeply connected relationships come easily to securely attached individuals. They give of themselves freely without living in constant fear of being taken advantage of by those they care about or abandoned. When they are tired, hungry, angry, stressed or overwhelmed, they have no problem sharing their feelings and asking for what they need. Securely attached individuals enjoy sharing the good times as well as the bad with their loved ones. They value being there for their partners in times of need and expect their partners to be there for them.

Many clients return angry to their next session after learning about their attachment style and that of their partner. They lament, "If only we had known this information a year ago we could have saved ourselves a lot of unnecessary suffering and avoided so many problems in our relationship!" Truer words have never been spoken.

Understanding attachment styles inevitably changes the energy around relationships. How we attach is neither good nor bad. It is what it is—like the color of your eyes. In the same way, we need to see our attachment style and therefore our needs around security, intimacy and availability as a fundamental part of who we are. Once we grasp this idea, we can begin to look at romantic relationships differently. Once we stop trying to become what the other person wants, accept ourselves for who we are and what our particular needs are, then we change the power dynamics in the relationship. We, rightly, switch from trying to figure out what we think this other person wants and focus on our own needs and if this person can meet our needs. Learning how you attach to others and they attach to you is a game changer in relational happiness. The significance of this internal dynamic is so important it is placed at the apex of the s.t.a.r.

9

INTERNAL FAMILY SYSTEMS

In 1913 sixty miles due west of Nashville, Tennessee, Lucius Murray Bowen was born to Jess and Maggie May Bowen. Bowen and his four siblings affectionately referred to their parents as Papa and Buh. Papa was a renaissance man. His various careers included farmer, entrepreneur and politician. As a tenant farmer, he was responsible for the land in exchange for half the crops. As an entrepreneur, he and his brother ran the local mercantile store when they weren't tending the farm. Papa became mayor of their rural community, which in the early 1900s consisted of approximately 1,100 souls.

Papa held a sacred love for family and the natural order of life. He taught his children the deep cycles of life, death, seasons, animals and crops. In a 1979 interview with Carl Whitaker, a co-pioneer with Bowen of the Family Systems model (not to be confused with Internal Family Systems), Bowen mused about his father:

> Dad was sort of determined that his kids would know the land. He put a tremendous amount of time with his sons hunting and fishing, inspecting crops, gathering nuts, explaining his built in knowledge of Nature, nursing sick animals, disposing of dead animals, assisting at the birth of animals, nursing homeless baby animals, training hunting dogs...watching animals' families and explaining their motives, watching fish swim and knowing what they were about.

After high school Bowen attended the University of Tennessee in Knoxville before being accepted to medical school at the University of Tennessee in Memphis. From 1941–1946 Bowen served in the Army where he trained for a future in surgery. However, his observations of the effects of war and trauma on soldiers, which later became known as Post-Traumatic Stress Disorder (PTSD), coupled with the deep wisdom of nature imparted to him by his father caused an internal shift toward healing the mind, not just the body. Always a trailblazer, Bowen reflected, "I gravitated toward the specialties that seem to offer the biggest unsolved problems."

Bowen went on to be one of the founders and leading thinkers in a model of therapy called Family Systems. His ideas on the structure of the mind subverted the established norms of the day by rejecting the Freudian psychoanalytic paradigm of family dynamics of repression and sexuality in favor of subjective experience and emotional attachment. In 1975 he founded the Georgetown University Family Center, which was later renamed Bowen Center for the Study of the Family. He remained director of the center he founded until his death in October of 1990.

Forty-seven years after Bowen was born, another trailblazing therapist entered this world on the cusp of one decade ending and another beginning. Richard Schwartz was an athletic youth who as a child became "addicted" to the game of basketball. One reason for the draw toward the sport was due to these transient, intense states of flow he experienced while playing. As he shuffled around on the basketball court, he found himself in the midst of experiences he later described as "blissful oneness." Schwartz writes of these almost mystical experiences being:[1]

> [F]leeting moments when I entered into a state in which my inner critics disappeared and my body seemed to know just what to do. I had total confidence in my abilities and experienced a sense of joy and awe at being spontaneously in the moment.

In 1967 Schwartz entered Knox College and studied psychology. Several years after graduation, he attended Northern

---
1 https://www.selfleadership.org/the-larger-self.html

Illinois University where he received his master's in community mental health. This was an interdisciplinary program consisting of psychology, sociology, counselor education and family therapy. It was here Schwartz trained in Bowen's model of treating familial dysfunction with Family Systems. Two years after graduate school, he was accepted to Purdue University where in 1980 he received his Ph.D. in marriage and family therapy.

Schwartz was a working academic. He coauthored textbooks and taught in the Department of Psychiatry at The University of Illinois at Chicago's Institute for Juvenile Research. He also worked with families and individuals struggling with eating disorders.

As many family therapists of his time, Schwartz drew upon his training in Family Systems for his clinical work. He found great success when working with families, but surprisingly, this did not translate to his work with individuals. Schwartz describes a moment that was not dissimilar from those moments on the basketball court so many years ago when the connection between thought and action started to foment into what would later become his life long work of *Internal Family Systems (IFS)*.

Schwartz credits his early eating disorder clients for triggering his awareness about parts. He recalls one in particular named Diane who described her struggle with her eating disorder. Schwartz said Diane shared with him her internal conversations that kept her in the binge/purge cycle. Diane said her pessimistic voice told her she was hopeless. When Schwartz inquired about the reason for its pessimism, the voice answered that if she feels hopeless she won't take risks and if she doesn't take risks she won't get hurt. But Diane had another part that hated the pessimist, and it was very angry. When asked why this other part was so angry, it responded by detailing how the pessimistic part makes decisions in her life an epic struggle.

In a moment of creative professional desperation, he sought any way possible to help his clients heal and make progress. He used what he knew best, which was his extensive training and experience with Family Systems, and applied it to the inner life of his clients with eating disorders.

It was obvious for Schwartz to see how his family therapy clients were made up of a system of different parts (e.g., mother, father, son, daughter, grandma, etc.) because those parts were actual people. Yet as he listened to what his clients were telling him, it felt like they had different parts inside them as well that often disagreed with other parts. This was very similar to his experience when working with family members who often disagreed with one another in sessions. Schwartz has dedicated nearly three decades to understanding and refining his *Internal Family Systems* model.

The idea of one person having multiple internal structures can be traced back to ancient Greece when Plato described the soul (psyche) as having three distinct parts: Logos (rationality), Eros (erotic love) and Thymus (desire). Sigmund Freud believed our minds were constructed of an id, ego and superego. Many of Shakespeare's characters, like Hamlet and Macbeth, engaged in arguments with different parts of themselves. Italian psychologist

Roberto Assagioli developed an approach called psychosynthesis in which he describes "subpersonalities." All of these dynamic approaches to understanding the mind are woven together with the same golden thread that we are not one monolithic personality. Rather, we are made of many different parts or subpersonalities.

One primary goal of IFS work is to help explore our vast array of parts as well as the *True Self*. Once we, as an autonomous rational being, gain an understanding of our many different parts, we can tend to them much like parents tend to their children. We can listen to each part with curiosity, care for each part with compassion and help each part face their fears with courage. We can help parts solve impossible problems through creative solutions. All of these actions bring a calming presence to the whole person that the *True Self* cares about each part and is in control. This benevolent leadership brings healing to the wounded parts and confidence to trust the *True Self*.

The *True Self* is an essence or energy present in each of us. It is altogether different than a part as it is a state of mind or way of being more than a psychological construct. Christians might refer to this as the soul. Hindus call this force atman. Muslims call it rūh. This force is what should be out front leading us, not the parts.

This universal guiding force expresses love to all parts through *Self Energy*. *Self Energy* is summarized in the 8 C's of *compassion, calm, curiosity, connected, clarity, creativity, confidence* and *courage*. IFS calls the practice of extending *Self Energy* to your parts *Self Leadership*.

Along with the 8 C's it is important to understand their opposites. It is in this paradox that most of our problems exist. Yet in a beautiful cycle of redemption, the problem ironically reveals the solution. If the problem is loneliness, the solution can be found in seeking connection. If the problem is a mind perpetually in chaos, then the solutions are to align with people who calm you and activities that restore your inner harmony.

Understanding and healing wounded parts is the primary work of IFS therapy. The *polarization* between parts is often what causes our impossible problems. When we are tasked with making a choice (e.g., staying in an unhealthy marriage for the kids or getting divorced), we have a part or sometimes many parts that are desperate to end the suffering and be free. However, there is another part or parts that want to subjugate our individual desires for the greater good of our children. This polarization causes major internal rifts among parts. If left to battle it out on their own, these parts will turn to unhealthy coping strategies, which will inevitably lead to depression, anxiety and, in the most extreme cases, psychosis and suicidal ideation.

Aristotle once noted that nature does nothing in vain. I would add that neither do our parts. Parts do not act randomly without reason. They have a purpose behind each and every action. This does not mean that every action is good or healthy. On the contrary, parts that are wounded or stuck or immature will often overreact to situations out of proportion to what would normally be expected. This predictably causes more problems than it solves.

Everyone's parts have a fatal flaw I call *The Tyranny of Now*. Each part feels whatever crisis it is experiencing RIGHT NOW is the most important thing, and it must be addressed immediately. If only our parts arranged themselves in an orderly line, each patiently waiting their turn to air their concerns to the *True Self*, life would be so much easier. But a more appropriate analogy of the incessant internal chatter of parts that are triggered is the chaotic hallways of any high school in between classes.

One of the functions of the *True Self* is to evaluate the tyrannical fears of a triggered part to determine if they are truly important and urgent or if they can be addressed later. The *True Self* must be aware that a parts, hyperbolic reactionary response to being triggered will, if not attended to in a compassionate, calm manner, hijack any moment.

What does it look like for a person to have a healthy Internal Family System? Here is an example. It is the end of a very long workweek when Charlotte gets a last-minute text from a guy asking her on a date. On the drive home, a debate erupts among her parts. Charlotte has a part she calls **The Romantic** who is very excited: "I've been wanting to go out with this guy for weeks!" Charlotte also has a very strong **Independent Woman** part. This part of her could take or leave dating at this point. She's working on saving the world and building a career. The **Independent Woman** throws a bucket of cold water on the situation, "Yeah, yeah, hold on a minute. Why didn't he ask sooner? By the way, he texted instead of calling. Rude." **The Romantic** knows how persuasive the **Independent Woman** can be and defends her territory, "Get with it, girl! That's the way it is these days. And besides he's SOOO cute!"

A third part, the one that hates it when the other parts fight, just wants to **Chill Out**. This part throws her two cents in with a warm sing-songy voice that drives the **Independent Woman** crazy, "Hey, ladies, why don't we just stay home and watch Netflix? That new show we've been waiting for premieres tonight!"

The debate rages all the way home. Finally, while sitting in her driveway Charlotte decides to accept the invitation. The **Independent Woman** reluctantly agrees. However, she puts **The Romantic** on notice. Anything less than chivalry from this guy and he's a goner.

This is an example of a healthy dialogue among parts and how polarization can be normal and healthy. Each part truly believes their perspective is the "right" one, yet many times they want something different. One part wants to go on the date, another part is put off by the suitor's sophomoric behavior and yet another part has an entirely different perspective of resolving the conflict—avoid it by staying home!

Even if Charlotte were to let the clock run out on making a decision, she is still making a decision. In these situations, one (or more) of her parts will be disappointed because they didn't get their way. If those parts are really angry, they will protest (e.g., throw a temper tantrum, get depressed, lash out, have a panic attack, drink to excess, cut themselves, eat a carton of ice cream, call an old boyfriend for a late-night hookup, etc.).

One of the most powerful qualities of IFS is its "nonpathological" orientation. Internal Family Systems doesn't see the client as sick/bad/wrong/broken/a diagnosis. IFS encourages a high degree of mindfulness and self-awareness and deeply believes that each individual possesses all they need to solve their own problems.

Let's return to Charlotte to see this one-for-all, all-for-one teamwork in action. **The Romantic** knows she will never find Mr. Right sitting at home watching reruns of HBO's *Girls*. The **Independent Woman** has no interest in dating "man boys," as she calls them, who don't have the decency to pick up the phone and ask a girl out. Based on the last guy, who turned out to be a total loser, her early warning lights are already flashing with the latest guy, ready to spot any behavior she might deem below her standards.

Remember, all of your parts want something good for you. **The Romantic** is eager and impetuous (and sometimes naïve) as lovers tend to be. The **Independent Woman** is strong and confident but can also be harsh at times and inflexible. She likes to lead but will, on occasion, reluctantly follow. She is smart enough to know she doesn't know everything. It is a challenge for her to tolerate the impetuousness of **The Romantic**. Truth be told the **Independent Woman** only wants the best for everyone involved. The **Chill Out** part just wants to relax.

Imagine your life as a bright flowing ribbon of light starting from the moment of your birth. This little ribbon of light flows freely until you experience some event that emotionally wounds you. This painful experience causes your once free-flowing ribbon of light to become a tangled constellation of energy like a knot in a rope. Your free-flowing life comes to a sudden stop as you attempt to untangle the knot.

However, just as you are making progress on your knot, you get wounded again and a new knot emerges. You leave the first tangled ball of energy to work on this new knot. Before long you get hurt again and then again. Before you know it, your once free-flowing ribbon of light becomes a bunch of tangled knots. These wounds are messy, but they are also sacred. Each wound represents the hard (and often unfair) work we are burdened with in this life.

Because of the ways in which we are uniquely wounded, our parts develop strategies to protect us from suffering. As we saw previously, when we hone these strategies they become automatic responses we no longer think about. These automatic loops play effortlessly on repeat. However, these loops will eventually fail us, and we must choose to either repress what once worked, but no longer works, or face the pain and learn the lesson buried in the mountain of misery. The cycle of pain/suffer/hide/repeat is a negative loop. This humiliating cycle isolates us and will eventually cause us to collapse physically and mentally. Until we do the hard work of understanding how parts of our painful past are still present in us today, we will continually repeat unhealthy patterns, which inevitably lead to further breakdowns.

There are times when the work we must do to resolve our problems becomes overwhelming. Our parts get stuck and slip into hopelessness and exhaustion. It feels like too much, or we simply don't know what to do. In this weary state, we may be tempted to abandon our wounded parts, hoping the passing of time will somehow miraculously fix what is broken.

The problem with repressing and exiling our hurting parts from our conscious life is that they don't go away; they simply descend into our unconscious where our ego loses control. This defense mechanism inevitably leads to more problems down the road with anxiety, depression or worse. The reason we fall into the trap of repressing our most painful thoughts is because it gives us temporary relief in the moment.

Saul McLeod writes in his article "Defense Mechanisms" about the strategies Sigmund Freud and his daughter Anna observed in how we cope with impossible problems:[2]

> Memories banished to the unconscious, or unacceptable drives or urges do not disappear. They continue to exert a powerful influence on behavior. The forces, which try to keep painful or socially undesirable thoughts and memories out of the conscious mind, are termed defense mechanisms.

Here is a sample of a few of Freud's coping strategies:

1. **Repression** – a tool used by our ego to prevent harmful thoughts from rising to our conscious mind. Freud's

---

[2] https://www.simplypsychology.org/defense-mechanisms.html

famous Oedipus Complex of repressing aggressive thoughts toward the same-sex parent is an example.

2 **Denial** – If repression is about thoughts, denial is keeping events in our life tucked away out of awareness. Cigarette smoking is undeniably linked to increased rates of cancer. However, a person may deny this or believe it won't happen to them.

3 **Projection** – Getting its name from the way films are projected onto screens, we project onto others what we find unacceptable in ourselves. For example, we might be overweight but criticize overweight actors on television for not having more self-control.

4 **Displacement** – Expressing an impulse like anger toward a person or object that is not the source of the intense emotion. An example of this would be someone who is angry at their boss by coming home and yelling at the children for playing too loud.

5 **Regression** – Regressing to an earlier, less mature state of development due to stress. If you get into an argument with your husband or wife, you act like a child by stomping around, making faces and ignoring them for days.

6 **Sublimation** – Substituting an unhealthy impulse like aggression in a healthy way. There is no better example than sports to describe how contemporary men and women feel the rush of intense emotion by yelling and screaming at an inanimate electronic box.

Parts in extreme roles are obvious. We cry when our child leaves for school because we have an irrational fear they might be kidnapped. We might yell at employees for making minor mistakes. We may ruthlessly pick and judge our partner's every move, making them feel as if they are inept.

Why would our parts engage in such ruthless behavior? What good could possibly come from making others feel bad? The truth is that many times our parts hold *outdated assumptions* and/or *false beliefs* about situations or people. This is often the fuel that powers the engine of extreme behaviors.

A *false belief* might be when you believe you are "not that smart" based on the fact that growing up you were mocked by your father and teased by your siblings. You became the butt of family jokes with hurtful mischaracterizations like, "Did you see what Henry just did. He is as dumb as a rock." There was no room for you to make normal mistakes kids make without being overly scrutinized, criticized and ridiculed. After hearing this lie for so long and suffering through childhood depression and weight issues, your grades slipped and you began isolating yourself. This painful story confirms in your mind that you are indeed "stupid." You internalize this false belief and carry it into adulthood.

An *outdated assumption* is something that may have been true at one point but is no longer true. During your senior year of college, you often drank to excess and would go into blind rages when even slightly offended. You were labeled a jerk and rightfully so. After getting into a near-fatal car accident while drunk, you sobered up literally and figuratively. Now you are more humble and keep the jerk part of you in check while trying to understand this part and move it toward its noble purpose. You extend compassion, courage and discipline to yourself by committing to Alcoholics Anonymous weekly and sponsoring five other men. Yet from time-to-time the old voices come back about how much pain you caused, opportunities you missed and how cruel you were to people. The *outdated assumption* is that you are still an out-of-control alcoholic and a jerk, both of which are no longer true.

If we allow one part to lead, we are elevating the priorities of one part of us to the exclusion of and above the others. This has dire consequences for the psyche. When we lead from an unhealthy part, we do things like making inappropriate sexual advances, feigning suicidal gestures for attention or making verbally or physically aggressive threats to people we care about. Unhealthy, aggressive parts such as these reject more thoughtful, sensitive parts because they make them feel weak and vulnerable.

For many people, their *True Self* is allusive. Parts are on display all the time every day in grand fashion. Anytime there is a strong emotion, positive or negative, that is a part trying to get your attention. The intended role of every part is to be an advisor to the *True Self*. However, if the part holds false beliefs based on incorrect information or painful unhealed wounds, the messages from a part can get warped and cause harm.

Initially in the place of healthy *Self-To-Part* relationships, there are often a plethora of tense *Part-To-Part* relationships. I often ask clients, "How do you feel toward the part of yourself that binges on food and alcohol when you're lonely?" They immediately respond, "I hate it!" which is understandable. The *Athletic* part feels sabotaged by the *Overindulgent, Coping-With-Food* part. They are *polarized* from each other. They both want to feel happy but have very different methods for achieving that goal.

As *True Self* brings a nonjudgmental attitude, *Self Leadership* emerges through *Self Energy* expressed through the 8 C's:

CALM
CLARITY
COURAGE
CURIOSITY
CREATIVITY
CONFIDENCE
COMPASSION
CONNECTEDNESS

The coping with food part nor the healthy, striving part is intended to run your life. *True Self* is intended to partner with all your parts. *True Self* is the only force with the patience and authority to lead the whole system thoughtfully, mindfully and impartially without judgment. *True Self* doesn't bring harsh, critical energy to the coping with food part for wanting to feel better and using food to accomplish its goal. *True Self* feels curiosity and compassion with a desire to connect and understand. Its desire is to move each part toward its intended healthy role of finding pleasure and satisfaction from food while not putting the body at risk.

Take Riley for instance. Riley came to see me in a panic. Earlier in the day after returning from her morning break, she found a large bouquet of flowers on her desk. Being her birthday, she wasn't terribly surprised but assumed they were from her boyfriend John. As she read the card, a part of her felt immense dread once she realized they were from her previous boyfriend. It was their dysfunctional relationship that initially brought her to therapy.

After more than a year, she finally felt healed from his neglectful behaviors. Now without warning, the flowers brought up a mixed bag of emotions she was not prepared to address. In a panic, she picked up the phone to call her boyfriend but realized she was too emotional to have a rational conversation. This information would upset him, but there would be nothing for him to do. She remembered our discussion of her parts and the 8 C's. She pulled the card from her purse with the 8 C's written on it and went for a walk.

As she let the sun bathe her face, she closed her eyes and asked herself what it might feel like to bring calm, curious *Self Energy* into this situation instead of aggressive energy. Her anxiety faded slightly as she acknowledged that a part of her still had feelings for her ex-boyfriend. She told herself this was understandable and was grateful to be aware they still existed because now she could work with them to improve her relationship with John.

She wanted to be fully present in her current relationship, and that would require her to understand these feelings on a deeper level. She retrieved her phone from her pocket and called to set an appointment with me. Once that was done, she returned to investigating which parts were feeling what emotions. She felt compassion for her ex-boyfriend knowing that he was a decent man but they made a bad pair. He most likely didn't have any ill will in his gesture of sending flowers. She assumed he was probably lonely. She was the one to break it off, and she'd heard through mutual friends that he was still not over her.

Riley knew there were a few parts of her that still wanted things to work out between them, yet she knew the most healthy decision is to be crystal clear with him that they are finished. She took out her phone again and wrote a brief text, "Steve, I received your flowers today. Thank you for the thoughtful gesture on my birthday. I want to be clear that I no longer have feelings for you and would appreciate no further contact. I wish you the very best in love and life."

Riley was beginning to feel calmer and more confident that she could handle this unexpected intrusion. Feeling the 8 C's flowing freely, she looked at her card and read through each one to see how they could be utilized in this situation. She stopped on creativity. She honored the part of her that wanted to toss the flowers in the garbage out of anger, but they were beautiful and it would be a shame to waste them.

After a few frustrating minutes without any inspiration, she suddenly remembered her friend Nancy in Human Resources. Her mother passed away last week after a prolonged illness. Instead of throwing the flowers away, she made a plan to wait until Nancy left her office for lunch. She would write an anonymous note of condolence and place them on her desk.

There are as many ways to experience parts as there are people. Schwartz, the founder of IFS, reports that he has only a vague sense of his parts. Others have strong bodily awareness of their parts. I tend to "see" my parts acting out scenes much like watching a TV show.

The motivation for establishing healthy *Self-To-Part* relationships are to:

1. Create harmony among all your parts to more effectively solve impossible problems, handle unexpected crises, prevent unnecessary suffering and prosper in life and relationships,

2. Heal parts that carry past wounds by unburdening those parts that are stuck in the past and bringing them into the present. In the present, they no longer need to relive the trauma where they were stuck. They can authentically let go of the need to continually relive the painful experience.

Healing is a normal, natural part of life. If you cut your hand while slicing a tomato, you clean it, put a bandage on it and in several days the wound is healed with maybe a small scar.

Emotional healing can happen in much the same way when given the right conditions. Beginning to see yourself in parts is a big leap forward in understanding how to heal your mind and unburden your wounded parts.

Remember, every solution to every problem you will ever have must begin with awareness. Until you clearly see the problem, it is difficult to solve it. Healing wounded parts takes time and intentional effort. This process must begin with understanding that you are made up of parts. In IFS you never have to go looking for what to work on. Any time you feel a strong emotion, that is a part trying to get your attention. *That* is what you need to work on.

As you get familiar with each part through strong emotional reactions, you will grow more comfortable dialoguing with them on a regular basis. So often when we feel strong emotions like anger, jealousy or sadness, we say things like, "I am mad" or "I am jealous," which implies all of you feels this way. That is rarely, if ever, true. Remembering to use the phrase, "A part of me feels..." when you encounter strong emotions will serve as a reminder that it is only part of you, not all of you.

As you make intentional efforts to get to know your many parts, they will begin to feel heard and seen. By hearing and seeing your parts, you are creating a safe, sacred space inside yourself. The deepest desire of any wounded part is for *True Self* to witness their stories. As Maya Angelou said, "There is no greater agony than an untold story."

INTERNAL FAMILY SYSTEMS

Your parts need your True Self to witness what they have endured. They need you to understand that when they get triggered, they are stuck in the past reliving painful memories in the present. Once a part can let go of the burden it has been carrying since the offense, it can freely live in the present. As this witnessing occurs, parts will spontaneously heal. This unburdening plays a part in revealing the intended, healthy role of each part.

I do not know for certain, but if I had to guess I would say Elizabeth Gilbert, author of *Eat, Pray, Love* and *Big Magic*, most likely had an IFS-trained therapist. I base this assumption on a quote from a 2016 interview with Krista Tippett on her *On Being* podcast. Gilbert explains:[3]

> And I see self-loathing everywhere I look in so many different forms. And it's so — it breaks my heart. And I also know self-loathing because I have been in it. Anybody who's been in depression knows what self-hatred is. In many ways, depression is — the best definition of it is anger turned inward. So, there's this battle that's going on within you where you become a rival of yourself and an enemy of yourself. And what transformed my life about that journey that I took with Eat, Pray, Love were those four months that I spent in India where I had to be alone with myself, and we really made a peace accord. And when I say myself, I should say my selves. Because we're not a self, we're selves.

---

3 https://onbeing.org/programs/elizabeth-gilbert-choosing-curiosity-over-fear/

And one by one, I really went around to all my selves and we shook hands and made peace with each other and said, "We're not going to operate against each other anymore. This has got to be a better neighborhood to live in. [laughs] We have to put down the weapons. We have to put down the old complaints. We have to put down the perfectionism. We have to put down the judgment. We have to put this stuff away because we're doing such tremendous harm to this poor being, Liz, who has to carry this war around within her.

PART 2

THE 8 C'S

10

THE 8 C'S

Impossible problems feel impossible because for all the days, weeks, months and sometimes years we have labored with them, we perpetually come up empty-handed without acceptable answers. It is necessary to remember in these exhausting loops that you always have options. Always. Even if those options are terrible/dreadful/awful. We must never relinquish one of our most fundamental privileges, which is our ability to choose a path and pursue it with enthusiasm.

Remembering we have choices is easy to forget when faced with impossible problems. We may despise the options in front of us, but that doesn't mean none exist. What we are really saying is that we don't like our options. We know if we follow through on them they will cause major disruptions in our life. Truth be told, many times we are not yet willing to make the tremendous sacrifices necessary for what we say we want.

In every session I am asking each client either overtly or covertly what Mary Oliver asks in her poem, *The Summer Day*, "Tell me, what it is you plan to do with your one wild and precious life?"

The 8 C's are an elegant approach to resolving impossible problems. Yet like most time-tested wisdom, they do not offer exact instructions on what to do. Rather they offer us something better: how to be. They instruct us how to act with courage, how to live with integrity and how to treat others and ourselves with compassion in the midst of difficult situations.

The 8 C's are positive, affirming qualities. Yet each of these qualities has a shadow just like each of us has a dark side. In Jungian psychology, the shadow contains the unacceptable urges and desires that get pushed aside. It is the antithesis of what we project to the world. Take, for example, a woman who wears lacy floral print dresses with sensible pumps, a delicate cross necklace and a warm, welcoming smile no matter her mood. This prim and proper façade is not fake, but neither is it the totality of this woman's psyche. Beneath her manufactured veneer lives unrealized versions of herself. Maybe one buried persona wears a leather jacket, rides a motorcycle, has a mean resting bitch face and chain smokes. This rabble-rouser answers to no one. Maybe another hidden shadow self is a sexy salsa dancer who wears lots of makeup and low-cut dresses that expose her undulating body. These characters were never manifested for a hundred sensible reasons, yet this woman's shadow exists.

We all have a shadow, and under certain circumstances this shadow can sneak past our best defenses. When it does escape, it wreaks havoc on our nicely manicured life.

Our shadow self is the antithesis of our manufactured self. It is a necessary yet destructive character. Think of the adage you can't have cold without the relativity of heat. You can't have light without the presence of darkness. In the same way, each of the 8 C's has a shadowy opposite we must acknowledge if we are to overcome our weaknesses and thrive.

The opposite of the 8 C's are like the tail fin of a weather vane. The wind whips and twirls the spindly post until the vane finds an equilibrium whereby the headwind brings it into alignment. The tip of the vane points into the wind. But the tail of the vane is also pointing in the exact opposite direction. This is the role of each of the antonyms of the 8 C's—to signal when we are going in the opposite direction of growth and maturity.

The antonyms serve as a valuable shadow. Unless we are living in total denial, most of us can sense when something isn't quite right in our lives. The eight antonyms give specific guidance on what direction we need to go once we identify where we are struggling.

The 8 C's are a healthy way to orient our thoughts and actions. They are also a path to pursue when trying to solve impossible problems. Living the opposite of the 8 C's may be necessary to learn valuable lessons, but they are ultimately unhealthy and cause unnecessary suffering. I will repeat this again and again: Staying too long in a bad thing is a bad thing that leads to other bad things and prevents good things from happening.

COMPASSION VS. APATHY

One form of compassion[1] is the ability to open one's self to the suffering of others. To be open to suffering is accepting suffering in others and ourselves as a fact. In accepting it, we want to understand what is causing the suffering, what can be learned from it, how to heal from it and help to alleviate it whenever appropriate and possible. Compassion includes the qualities of kindness, empathy, generosity and acceptance. Compassion is the acknowledgement that not all pain can be fixed or solved, but all suffering is made more approachable through the lens of compassion. Compassion is the foundation upon which

[1] http://ccare.stanford.edu/research/wiki/compassion-definitions/compassion/

all the other "C" words are grounded. Courage without compassion is reckless. Confidence without compassion is conceited and so on.

A question I ask clients as they begin naming their parts is, "How do you feel toward the part of you that is causing you distress right now?" The response I hear most often is, "Ugh! I hate it!" or "That part is so weak it disgusts me."

Parts work focuses primarily on parts that are triggered and/or polarized from other parts. Conversely, we have healthy parts that do not need this type of attention and intervention. When a part is triggered, it is expressing its unhappiness by protesting in the form of disrupted sleep and lack of appetite. These are attempts by parts to gain attention. The triggered parts may resort to causing panic attacks seemingly out of the blue.

Such harsh responses from parts are normal. Don't we all hate things that make us feel bad? Before we recognize these are just parts that need healing and not enemies to be destroyed, we see these parts as hell-bent on our destruction. We must destroy them before they destroy us. If we look to our recent past, we see examples of how these parts have caused us no small amount of suffering. When was the last time you couldn't fall asleep or once awake couldn't go back to sleep due to worrying? Yet even in our suffering, these parts are only trying to bring us something they think we need.

What I now know when I hear this "I hate it!" criticism of another part is that their *True Self*, the essence of who they are, would never say such cruel things about a part.

Based on that assumption, I know I am talking to another part, not their *True Self*. I also know it is my job to help this client understand that this critical voice is just one part's opinion of another part.

Many parts naturally oppose other parts for the simple reason that these other parts stand in the way of them accomplishing their goal. They will use whatever method necessary to overpower the part that opposes their agenda. In truth, wouldn't you want it that way? If you were lost in the woods and were absolutely convinced you knew the way out, but another member of your pack was equally convinced that a different direction was the way out, wouldn't you argue pretty fiercely for your opinion? If you were truly convinced you were right, wouldn't you consider heading out on your own and leaving the group behind?

What is the best course of action in this never-ending cycle of part-to-part drama? Allow your *True Self* to offer all parts involved compassion. It is helpful to simply acknowledge how hard each part is working, some of them to the point of exhaustion and sickness. If the only tool a client learns in therapy is to identify their parts and extend compassion to each part, I would consider therapy a success. This one step alone is an epic leap toward self-understanding, healing and happiness.

Think about a time when a friend or family member was hurting and you extended them compassion in their moment of grief. What happened? They softened. They opened up. They may have even allowed themselves to break down further because they felt safe in your presence.

That is all someone needs in order to begin healing the damage of an all too often cruel world. This need not be a rare event. This can be a daily, and sometimes hourly, practice.

If you were to practice compassion toward yourself and others on a daily basis, it would have a radical impact on your life, those in your sphere of influence and to some degree the whole world. This practice would make your relationships richer, your work more meaningful and your love more expansive. Lest this portrayal come across as hyperbolic, let me add that profound strength and discipline are required to extend and receive compassion.

But what of compassion's shadow, apathy?

I remember in my early twenties when I first heard someone say that apathy is the opposite of love, not hate. The idea disturbed me. As I sat with it, I remember having a dawning awareness that when you hate someone it is typically because they aren't giving you something you want. They broke up with you. They didn't parent you well. They fired you. But when you feel apathy toward someone, you lack compassion toward them and their well-being. You do not care if they live or die. You do not care if they suffer. You would not lift a finger to help them or even harm them. You truly could not care less.

Apathy is indifferent to the suffering of others. One of the most destructive elements of apathy is its lack of willingness to see the other and engage them. I often remind clients that if they want something new and different in their life they must create a space for it. Creating a space for something new demands energy and attention.

Helen Keller once observed, "Science may have found a cure for most evils; but it has found no remedy for the worst of them all—the apathy of human beings." Why would anyone ever choose apathy over compassion? If everything we do is to make ourselves happy, why would we choose an anti-emotion over an actual emotion? It is because of the fatal flaw of the tyranny of now.

It is a highly advanced way of being to live in the present moment with mindful self-awareness. It is an entirely opposite experience to live apathetic in the present moment without self-awareness. Many people direct apathy toward themselves, their spouse, their children and their work because it requires less of them.

What can you do if you find yourself apathetic toward your career? How can you save your marriage if you feel apathy toward your spouse? First, you must diligently seek out the embers of desire (and trust me, they are there somewhere) and fiercely protect them. Once you realize that you are not the living dead and there is still hope within, you must create a space with time, intention and energy for something new. Even if you have to "fake it till you make it," when it comes to compassion that works just fine. In other words you can back your way into compassion. Act compassionately toward yourself and others, and the feeling will follow.

The Greater Good Center at the University of California, Berkley writes on their website:[2]

> While cynics may dismiss compassion as touchy-feely or irrational, scientists have started to map the biological basis of compassion, suggesting its deep evolutionary purpose. This research has shown that when we feel compassion, our heart rate slows down, we secrete the "bonding hormone" oxytocin, and regions of the brain linked to empathy, caregiving, and feelings of pleasure light up, which often results in our wanting to approach and care for other people.

Love, compassion, intimacy are words that come with baggage in our culture. Typical discussions about what it means to be a man don't include the terms compassion and intimacy. More often the language describing men is tough and domineering. Men *are* strong (because they have more testosterone in their system), but men are not *only* strong, testosterone-fueled animals. Through subtle (and sometimes, not-so-subtle) messaging, film, music, institutions like fraternities, sports and professions attempt to sideline the more compassionate virtues of man.

Whether it is overtly acknowledged or covertly spread by parents to their children, compassion is equated with weakness. The source of the dilemma with compassion is that we are rarely shown strong compassion. Parents are responsible for teaching us about compassion, but they are faced with two very disabling dilemmas. First, parents

---

2 https://greatergood.berkeley.edu/compassion/definition

are broken people too who were taught a bastardized form of compassion by broken people. It isn't possible to teach something to your children that you were never taught or never accurately learned. Second, the world is a harsh place, and parents fear that if their child is compassionate they will be taken advantage of by cruel, less compassionate people. True compassion is flexible to the context of a situation. Sometimes compassion looks tender and meek. Other times compassion is strong and brave, even violent.

The Buddhists have a teaching of compassion that embodies this flexibility. Robert Thurman, professor of Indo-Tibetan Buddhist Studies at Columbia University, summed up this philosophy in an interview on the *On Being* podcast:[3]

> [T]he Tibetans might prefer maybe the expression "fierce compassion." This is...where you don't indulge another person in their evildoing or their nasty behavior, and sometimes...have to be forceful. But that forcefulness with them will have a different impact, and it will be subliminally sensed by them as coming from a different place when it doesn't have that extra bite, that extra sting of hatred and vindictiveness in it. It's just forceful opposition to whatever negative things they are doing.
>
> So the psychology of "love your enemies" does not just mean, "Come and trample us. Come

[3] https://onbeing.org/programs/sharon-salzberg-robert-thurman-meeting-our-enemies-and-our-suffering/

kill me, my enemy. Oh, yes, I want you to shoot me," or something. It means, "I want you to be happy. I'm gonna be happy no matter what, and it's better. You'll be more happy if you don't kill me, actually. And I might be more happier if you don't kill me. But I'm gonna be happy, whatever you do to me. But on that basis, I might take your weapon away. I might be kung fu master or whatever. I might shoot you, actually, if you're about to shoot 150 other people. I might be forced. I try not to kill you, but I might be forced to do something forceful.

Breathwork specialist Max Strom offers sage advice on what compassion looks like in a practical way in his TED Talk titled *Breathe To Heal*. As expected, the first fifteen minutes of his lecture focuses on the benefits of breathwork. He made his case for the necessity of paying attention to our breath and how to maximize it to improve awareness and health. What is not expected is the gift he offers in the last few minutes of how to be with someone who is suffering in grief.

We are rarely prepared for tragedy. Trying to figure out what to say to someone shattered by loss can be agonizing. It is not uncommon to resort to silence and avoidance. Strom eloquently instructs us in this necessary skill of speaking compassionately into the unspeakable:

If we ask ourselves, "Why is this? Why do so many of us suppress grief?" It's because we're taught to. Mostly, in an unspoken way, we're taught that

COMPASSION VS. APATHY

expressing grief is socially unacceptable. If you think about it, we'll express anger much more readily than grief. We'll shout at the TV screen if our team is losing, we'll yell at another car and not apologize to the passengers in our car. But if you start crying when you're talking to someone, you'll wipe the tears away quickly and say, "I'm sorry, I don't know where that came from. I'm sorry." And especially men, we're taught, "Never let them see you cry. It's a sign of weakness and failure." So that's what we've been taught.

On top of that, no one ever taught us what to do when our friends are grieving, so we avoid them. On top of going through the grief event, our friends scatter, they don't know what to do, they've never been taught. They think they'll make us feel awkward, so they avoid us, and so now we're isolated as well. I think that if we came together, we would build stronger bridges of friendship, we would create more intimacy, and you don't have to say anything to someone who's grieving. Don't try to cheer them up. Just say, "It's going to hurt really bad for a while. I'm not going anywhere. I'm here. This year it's your turn. Next year it might be my turn. We'll all get through this together."

My profession offers many opportunities to be in the midst of deep suffering and grief, but even with all of my practice it is still not easy. To hold a space for sadness without trying to remove it is uncomfortable. This is one of the deepest forms of compassion we can extend to others...and ourselves.

A compassion brimming with tenderness and strength is the best *Self Energy* medicine you can extend to all of your parts whether they are wounded or not. Training yourself to bring compassion to your parts consistently will reap the rewards of less anxiety, less depression, more joy and more happiness.

12

COMPASSION IN ACTION

All the other 8 C's stand on compassion's shoulders. Without it, you cannot escape the abyss of narcissism.

What does compassion have to do with solving your impossible problems and finding lasting, authentic happiness? The Dalai Lama once remarked, "If you want others to be happy, practice compassion. If you want to be happy, practice compassion." When it gets right down to it, we all want to be happy. And there's absolutely nothing wrong with that.

Happiness gets a bad rap for being a transitory, throwaway emotion that we should shun in favor of more meaningful pursuits. Happiness has a lot to offer, and it has an excellent cost-to-benefit ratio. Most of us want to be happy with our work though many people despise their jobs. We go out with friends for "happy hour." We spend money on movies and an array of streaming cable and video services to escape our lives because that makes us happy. We go on vacations to relax and be happy.

Like all the other 8 C's, compassion is a skill that can be learned and, once learned, exercised regularly. If you already believe yourself to be a compassionate individual do not fret! You can become even more compassionate. You will run out of years on this earth before you reach the end of your potential to grow wiser and offer compassion.

Years ago there was a story circulating on Facebook about a man and his unruly children on the subway. The children were rambunctious, running around unattended and annoying other passengers. The father sat oblivious to his children's mayhem. Finally, an angry commuter confronted the hapless father about the behavior of his children. "I'm so sorry," the man said, "we just came from the hospital. Their mother died this morning after a long battle with cancer." Did your perspective shift once you understood the man lost his wife and the kids lost their mother? Did you immediately feel compassion for his situation?

Do not underestimate the transformational changes that can occur as you extend compassion to the unruly, problem-causing parts of yourself. There is very little to be gained by attacking them and everything to be gained by being kind.

Buddhists have a proverb when faced with an impossible problem: The only way out is through. When life requires you to army crawl on your hands and knees through hell, as we all are from time-to-time, giving yourself a little love along the way will get you farther faster than cruelty ever will. As Sharon Salzberg compassionately reminds us, "You yourself, as much as anybody in the entire universe, deserve your love and affection."

When you make compassionate, encouraging statements to yourself such as, "You can do this! Let's take it one step at a time" or "You are worth it! Keep going!" it infuses difficult moments with vitality.

On the contrary, negative, sarcastic comments like, "I'm such an idiot. Of course I failed. I deserve this." have the opposite effect. They drain the mind and soul of strength at critical moments when it is most needed.

Getting stuck on occasion is inevitable. Sometimes bad things happen for no identifiable karmic reason. The 8 C's are master skills designed to help you navigate when life is good and when it is bad, when there are no answers or when the only options are bad and worse, when we do not know what to do or no longer want to live.

The intentional, consistent practice of compassion leads to resilience that fortifies your life from the inevitable turbulence. Compassion also tethers the soul to a safe harbor when storms threaten. Compassion is an invaluable member of your inner life that will repay you a thousand times your investment.

How can you cultivate compassion?

In conjunction with Harvard University, Massachusetts General Hospital conducted a research study using an eight-week mindfulness-based meditation course and concluded:

> The analysis of MR images, which focused on areas where meditation-associated differences were seen in earlier studies, found increased gray-matter density in the hippocampus, known to be important for learning and memory, and in structures associated with self-awareness, compassion, and introspection.

In other words, when you practice meditation you are stimulating areas of the brain associated with compassion. That is why those areas become denser. Conversely, these same participants noted a marked decrease in stress:

> Participant-reported reductions in stress also were correlated with decreased gray-matter density in the amygdala, which is known to play an important role in anxiety and stress.

If you are the type that needs hard data, look no further. Mindfulness meditation is your go-to and is far simpler than you might imagine. For a ten-minute guided mindfulness meditation, go to rebbuxton.com/meditation. Here is a printed version of the online meditation. It may be helpful to read through these instructions to get familiar with them, then have a partner read them to you while your eyes are closed:

COMPASSION IN ACTION

1. Find a place where you will not be disturbed. Complete silence isn't necessary, but it is more productive if there are not people or animals coming in and out of your area. If they do, let them become part of your meditation. More on this below.

2. Sit up straight but not rigid in a chair or on a pillow on the floor. Refrain from listening to music. It will only distract you. If you want sound, experiment with Tibetan singing bowls or natural elements like babbling brooks or storms. Meditation is exercise. It is intended to raise awareness, not lull you to sleep. Also, if you lie down it is likely you will fall asleep.

3. Now close your eyes and bring attention to your feet by wiggling your toes. Move your awareness slowly up your body, noticing each distinct area of your body.

4. Bring attention to your calves, knees and thighs against the couch/chair/cushion. Relax your stomach, wiggle your fingers, relax your forearms, shoulders and let your arms hang heavy by your sides.

5. If it is comfortable, roll your neck around to relieve stress and tension.

6. Relax your eyes, your jaw, your lips.

7. Next take in a deep breath and exhale through your mouth. Notice where you feel your breath. Do you feel it in the back of your throat, chest or abdomen?

8. Breathe in again and notice where you feel the air coming in and what you notice in your body as you inhale.

9 Repeat steps 7 and 8 for ten minutes.

10 If you notice sounds around you (e.g., people talking, the chime of the elevator, a bird chirping, lawn mowers, car horns, chime/buzz of your phone, the click of a woman's heels on a hard floor, dogs barking, etc.), briefly make each sound the focus of your meditation. This lessens the energy of each distraction and utilizes their energy by incorporating them into your meditation. The logic is that during moments of focused calm during meditation, if you can be mindful of the distractions around you then let them go, you will be able to do the same in the stressful, anxious moments of everyday life.

11 Next—learn to notice your thoughts in a new way. How long did it take before your mind drifted to what you will eat for lunch or how your car needs an oil change or that email from a client that needs attention? The great moment of awareness is when you realize this thought has taken you away from your breath. This awareness IS meditation, not a failure to meditate. This is an extremely important point that many people misunderstand.

The point of meditation is not to clear your mind but to embrace the fact of how our minds constantly bombard us with information as we attempt to sit quietly and focus on our breath. You will *never* be able to clear your mind of distractions. The multitude of ways our minds get distracted is infinite. From something as mundane as an itch to something as complex as marital problems, our mind is constantly at work to solve our problems not be present to the moment. Naval Ravikant, founder of AngelList, calls this lack of presence either future-casting or past regretting. Learning to intentionally slow down and focus on the present is a muscle that must be exercised to achieve authentic happiness. This is why they call meditation a "practice."

As you consistently practice meditation, you will experience euphoric moments of awareness. When these occur you realize you don't have to let your thoughts rattle on incessantly out of your control. You can regain control at any moment as you mindfully choose what you want to think about. This may not sound like much of a revelation. However, if you are obsessing over a bad job interview or ruminating about an argument you had with your girlfriend for the hundredth time, it *is* a grand idea to give your mind permission to rest.

The Buddha used the analogy of a waterfall when describing the powerful inertia of our thought life. He said our thoughts are like a waterfall. If we mindlessly stand under a waterfall, we are going to get pummeled. Anyone who has stood beneath an actual waterfall will understand the accuracy of his analogy. The objective of meditation, the Buddha instructed, is to get behind the waterfall. You still see the rushing water in front of you, but you aren't being overwhelmed. During meditation the goal is to get distance from your thoughts, not be taken on a ride by the train of thought.

What are other ways to grow compassion? How you talk to yourself is one of the most overlooked yet powerful forces that shapes our daily life. This idea fits nicely alongside meditation because meditation helps you pay attention to thoughts as they manifest. To do this you first need to become aware of your inner voice and what it is saying.

I ask clients to tell me what it is like to live inside their head from the moment they wake up till they go to bed. How do they talk to themselves? When are they kind? Neutral? Harsh? Do they constantly criticize themselves? Whose voice it is? Their mother? Their father? Their favorite teacher from elementary? Their own voice?

Ponder this: What if your mind was your greatest asset? What if it didn't sabotage you with pessimistic thoughts about your body, your salary or feelings of unworthiness due to the way you were parented? What if your mind worked for you?

I once had a client, Samantha, whose mind was *not* her greatest asset. Every night before going to bed, she would mindlessly go about her bedtime routine. Her nightly ritual included washing her face, brushing her teeth and choosing her outfit for the next day. On the way from the bathroom to her bed, her routine included a vicious habit of standing in front of her full-length mirror and critiquing her body. The consequence of this mindless pattern was that she went to bed each night depressed and lonely believing that no one could love someone who looked like her. But the negative pattern didn't end with her going to bed. In the morning she stood in front of the same mirror and picked up where she left off the night before with sarcastic and critical insults.

Samantha was athletic in high school and played intramural sports in college. After law school, her job took precedence over self-care. Due to sitting behind her desk all day and working as much as seventy hours a week, she quickly gained a fair amount of weight. Living on little sleep, a poor diet and being overworked, she stopped going to the salon years ago to "save money."

Her commute to work each morning offered no respite from her inner critic. Every morning she heaped shame on herself for not waking up earlier and exercising. She made empty promises to do better tomorrow, knowing she would never keep them. The themes in all of her thoughtless routines were the same: I'm fat, I'm ugly and no one could ever love someone like me. Samantha subsisted on what I call *Junk Food For The Soul*. This diet of criticism and shame sabotaged any possibility of improving her self-esteem.

Most people pay no attention to the voices in their head. They believe the critical voice is a permanent installation that cannot be altered. The truth is, how you talk to yourself hour after hour, day after day, truly matters. Your internal dialogue, those voices in your head, create the air in which all parts breathe. If the atmosphere is toxic, your thoughts will be too. If your internal ecosystem is healthy, your thoughts will be healthy too. The not-so-secret secret is that you can clean up the atmosphere of your mind with intentional, directed effort. In return this atmosphere of compassion, curiosity and courage will manifest hope, optimism and joy.

Here are a few quick hacks to bring awareness to your thought life:

1. For the next seven days, set a reminder on your phone. When the alarm sounds, stop and write down the thoughts you are having about yourself in the moment or over the past few hours.
2. Do not turn on the television or radio in the morning while eating breakfast. Sit in silence and notice what comes up.
3. Drive to and from work in silence.
4. At the end of the night, journal about these experiences. See what you discover after a few days.
5. Create your own activities to raise your awareness of your inner dialogue.

These seemingly trivial actions may seem like overdone clichés. They may not produce any immediate solutions to your impossible problems. The objective here is to think and act differently so you can arrive at novel solutions and original ideas. In small but important ways, this is an example of how to go about the hard work of happiness.

Once clients truly begin to pay attention to the voices in their head, they suddenly recognize how unproductive much of the chatter tends to be. Dan Harris had this to say about the voices in his head during a talk he gave at Google Headquarters in New York, "It's like being kidnapped by the most boring person in the world. They keep saying the same thing over and over again."

One important myth to dispel is that these hypercritical voices are offering us the "unvarnished truth." We incorrectly believe these little critters running amok are the only ones willing to tell us the cold, hard truth about ourselves.

Samantha's inner critic told her that she was fat, ugly and no one could ever love her. The reality was that she was over her ideal weight, and her physical appearance was not up to par because she was not taking proper care of herself. However, to link those temporal circumstances to her worth as a woman was a tragedy.

The bigger question is why do we tell ourselves these things? Why would we want to sabotage our hope in such damaging ways? What could be the benefit of tearing ourselves down? Samantha's parts want her to exercise, look attractive, date, fall in love, marry, etc. But there are parts of her that have been deeply wounded by rejection from previous boyfriends, the pressure of society to conform to a thin, beautiful, confident stereotype while also maintaining a full-time job, working out every day at the gym, eating only edamame, kombucha and sushi...and...and...and.

Those parts of her that are not exercising and not tending to her appearance are trying to protect her. They don't trust men, and they loathe perpetuating unhealthy stereotypes of women based on shallow cultural values. They fear getting rejected again, and the best way to avoid rejection is to make themselves invisible. This fosters an attitude of hopeless pessimism, which creates inaction and isolation.

The extreme beliefs of these parts are that if they can keep her from taking care of her body and physical appearance, then she won't be tempted to go on dates. If she doesn't go on dates, no one can hurt her. There is less risk of rejection if they don't put themselves in situations to be rejected. What these wounded parts want more than a boyfriend is to never be hurt again. Wayne Gretsky was famous for saying, "You miss 100 percent of the shots you don't take." These frightened parts would rather deal with poor health, depression, hopelessness and despair than rejection, contempt and shame.

The good news is these parts with extreme beliefs do not represent her entire system. The other parts of Samantha are getting weary of being lonely and unhealthy and are starting to fight back. An example of how they are fighting for what they want is to convince Samantha to go to therapy, set healthy goals, take off a day from work to go to the spa, go out on weekends, etc.

When I figured out Samantha's daily and nightly routines, we began crafting creative, compassionate solutions to challenge her false beliefs and outdated assumptions. We did not shy away from the truth. She was over her ideal weight, and she had not been to the salon in over a year. I suggested she move the full-length mirror into the guest bedroom. If she wanted to look at herself, she would need to make an intentional effort, which would give her the opportunity to create a moment of mindfulness. I suggested she write on her full-length mirror, "My reflection is photons reflecting off of a smooth surface. It is not a measurement of my worth as a woman."

As Samantha started to become mindful through meditation, she began noticing throughout the day when she engaged in destructive self-talk. She devised her own strategy to replace negative rants with positive, truthful, affirming mantras. Research suggests it is more helpful when engaging in positive self-talk to use "you" instead of "I."[1] The researchers concluded that using "you" gives the mind the impression of talking to someone else, and we are always more forgiving and understanding with others than ourselves.

Samantha crafted her positive mantra to be, "Even though you are over your ideal weight and you have not been to the salon in over a year, you want to take care of yourself. When you lose ten pounds you will treat yourself to a day at the salon." I encouraged Samantha to read this daily and share her goals with her sister whom she trusts.

It was no magic bullet. She was successful at first, but after a few weeks she repeated her mantra less and less. As a result, she slipped back into old patterns. After several more weeks, she slipped into a melancholy state. However, instead of remaining there for months, her highly motivated parts wrestled her from her depression. She recommitted to her mindfulness practices, joined a fitness club and started running three times a week with a group for accountability.

Within a few short weeks, she lost ten pounds and met her first goal. She was astonished at how quickly she was able to lose weight once she fully committed to taking care of

[1] https://www.wsj.com/articles/self-talk-when-talking-to-yourself-the-way-you-do-it-makes-a-difference-1399330343

herself. How you talk to yourself is a true indicator of how much compassion you have for yourself.

How else can you practice compassion? When you stop reading this chapter, do two acts of compassion: the first toward yourself, the second toward someone else. The act of compassion toward yourself is to acknowledge your value to the world and how hard all of your parts are working to make your life a success. This proclamation is not about something external but your worth as a person.

The act of compassion toward someone else might be playing Legos with your kid when you would rather be watching the game, cooking dinner for friends, opening a door for a stranger and wishing them well on their day, giving money to a homeless person without worrying if they will use it for drugs, alcohol or food.

13

CALM VS. CHAOS

Chaos is the enemy of calm. Calmness is the antidote to chaos. But we shouldn't malign chaos as inherently bad. Anyone who has attended a child's birthday party that included an inflatable bouncy castle truly understands chaos...that is, until someone gets hurt and someone always gets hurt. Once the inevitable head bump/swollen lip/bloody nose occurs, everyone must calm down. Other forms of chaos can be beautiful, like a storm or seconds after a team wins the World Series.

Calmness is becoming harder to find in our modern, overly connected, geographically expanding society. I would gander that before harnessing electricity, when we went to bed at sunset, calm was abundantly possible to find and even problematic. Too much calm leads to boredom and...well...idle hands and all.

Today we must plan for calmness weeks and months ahead of time, hunting it down like an escaped convict. We attempt to find calmness on camping trips, spiritual retreats, during meditation, at the beach, those blissful moments underwater in the pool. We often find it accidentally when we are not looking for it in places like the hospital at night while sitting next to the bed of a loved one. We find it while watching our kids in bed as we check on them one last time. We find it in the morning before everyone else rises with our favorite mug full of hot coffee and the beautiful, hopeful sunrise.

It is difficult to remain calm when the only options to our impossible problems are bad or worse. Ryan Holiday suggests in *The Obstacle Is The Way*:

> [W]e can see opportunity in every disaster, and transform that negative situation into an education, a skill set, or a fortune. Seen properly, everything that happens—be it an economic crash or a personal tragedy—is a chance to move forward. Even if it is on a bearing that we did not anticipate.
>
> There are a few things to keep in mind when faced with a seemingly insurmountable obstacle. We must try:

- To be objective
- To control emotions and keep an even keel
- To choose to see the good in a situation
- To steady our nerves
- To ignore what disturbs or limits others
- To place things in perspective
- To revert to the present moment
- To focus on what can be controlled

The quote above is about seeking out and remaining calm in the midst of chaos. It often feels as if there is an ongoing war between calm and chaos at every turn. Blink and your yard will overtake your house if you don't beat it back with a lawn mower and hedge trimmer. Blink again and you will overshoot the monthly data limit on your family mobile phone sharing plan, skyrocketing your bill to hundreds of dollars above normal. Blink yet again while texting on your phone and you'll get T-boned at the intersection just blocks from your front door.

Calmness is one of the easiest to overlook of the 8 C's. In our fast-paced, high-tech world, a significant news event can circumnavigate the globe before we've had our morning coffee. We are never far from access to some form of tragedy.

Calm brings perspective. Being calm when things are good is easy. Remaining calm in the midst of an injustice, tragedy or when others lose their head is a real challenge. However, learning this skill is the difference between success and everything else.

To be calm you must have an understanding of how your mind is organized *and* your body's natural, healthy response to stress. Enter the Vagus nerve.

The Vagus nerve and the amygdala connect near the base of the brain. The amygdalae are buried deep in the primal core of the brain with one in each hemisphere. The amygdalae are central to the systems related to memory, decision-making and emotional responses. From deep within, the Vagus nerve travels from the base of the skull down each side of the neck and throat where it enters the chest, heart and lungs, making its way to the stomach, liver, intestines and other major organs. The Vagus nerve constitutes a major portion of the autonomic nervous system, which is the seat of the fight-or-flight response.

When your nervous system gets triggered by an event like a child running out into the street in front of your car, the amygdala sends a signal via the Vagus nerve to release adrenalin, cortisol and a host of other stress hormones. This response catapults your body into an intense physical reaction that shocks the body. It physically feels terrible, but this is your body functioning properly.

In addition to the typical fight-or-flight response there is a third state known as freeze. When frozen in a traumatic situation, either real or imagined, the mind sends the body the same fight-or-flight signal. However, if we are reliving something from the past in the present, there is nothing to run away from. It is a false positive. As Bessel van der Kolk says, "The past is over and done with. You can't do anything about it. What matters is how alive the past is in your body today."

Once the warning bells have sounded, the body's job is to respond as if there is an actual threat. The chain reaction of stress hormones floods the system, creating an unbearable sensation. The watchtower part of the brain, the medial prefrontal cortex, goes into hyper-drive and scans everything and everyone believing, "There must be a threat somewhere. I just have to find it!" This misguided hypervigilance begins a cascade of negative chain reactions such as acute stress, high blood pressure, anxiety, panic attacks, anxiety attacks, depression, mood swings, dissociation, violent outbursts, self-harm, etc.

Sharon was a 28-year-old client in a very bad relationship. Her boyfriend was shrewd enough never to leave marks on her, but he would psychologically manipulate her in ways that made her feel as if she were losing her mind—a phenomenon known as gaslighting. Some of his deceptive strategies included hiding her birth control and emotionally manipulating her into having sex. These attempts were made in an effort to get her pregnant whereby she would never be free of his grasp. He went so far as to create fake email accounts of men and send racy emails from those accounts to her phone. He would search her phone and accuse her of cheating.

Once he locked her in a closet for a day without food, water or her phone. She was fired from her job, which created more of a dependence on him. She had few living family members, none of whom lived nearby. Since dating him, most of her close friends had drifted away or were intimidated by his threatening behavior toward them. She eventually escaped when he spent 30 days in jail for multiple drunk driving offenses.

She moved near her family and cut off all contact with him. It took her years before she could date again. Most of those relationships ended prematurely. None of these men could endure her unpredictable mood swings, paranoia and codependency. She never trusted these men enough to share the real reasons behind her actions. This resulted in them seeing her as mentally unstable instead of a survivor of domestic violence with Post-Traumatic Stress Disorder (PTSD) and recovering from psychological abuse.

None of the threatening scenarios in her new relationships presented actual threats. These men were healthy, for the most part, who occasionally made mistakes or lost their temper. However, every day, Sharon carried with her memories of her past trauma. When she perceived the slightest threat, her amygdala overreacted by sounding the alarm of, "DANGER! Get Away Now! He will lock you in the closet!" These signals told her she needed to escape or something terrible would happen. However, her logical brain knew there were no actual threats. Her post-traumatic stress reactions were confusing to her suitors and ultimately proved unsustainable for them. Her emotional brain and logical brain were not working in unison. Her emotional brain kept hijacking her body, refusing to let her enjoy simple pleasures like holding hands or kissing.

If you have been traumatized in past relationships through betrayals or unsafe situations and have not reconciled those experiences in a meaningful way, the potential to bring those past experiences into your current relationship is unavoidable. If you are in a bad relationship and do not feel safe, it is imperative you make decisions necessary to feel safe. Remember, staying too long in a bad thing is a bad thing that leads to more bad things and prevents good things from happening. To reconcile past trauma with your current reality requires that your body and mind work together. When they are not working in unison, they create post-traumatic responses that interrupt the healthy flow of life, spread fear and kill joy.

The humiliating experience of reliving past trauma in the present is prominent with big "T" Traumas like car accidents, untimely deaths of loved ones and divorces. However, overwhelming sensations of fear, panic and anxiety happen with little "t" traumatic events as well. Mark Epstein calls these the traumas of everyday life. These include breakups, unexpected job loss, financial stress, a neglectful spouse or simply watching the news day after day. Often we experience these traumas simultaneously.

The take-home message about the Vagus nerve and fight, flight or freeze is that your body is not the problem; it is only a messenger sending a message. It is the unhealed psychological parts sending the warnings that are causing stress, fear and anxiety. Do not shoot the messenger.

When you suppress your emotions to be able to function in daily life, you do not get to choose which emotions get exiled. In other words, it is not possible to exist in a numb state of emotional repression and feel happiness, joy and love.

Sharon shared with me how after many terrible interactions with her boyfriend she learned not to say anything that could be interpreted by him as annoyance or anger. She had to continually be perky, upbeat and non-confrontational around him. She said she was afraid to be honest with him out of fear that he would retaliate by verbally assaulting her. She described how on one long car trip she asked to stop and use the restroom. They had stopped an hour before, but she had an upset stomach and needed to go to the restroom again. She said he became so irate with her request that she feared he might wreck the car. He refused to stop, and in her terror she defecated on herself.

After that event, whenever she felt anger toward him she chose to "stuff it." "Eventually," she said through a forced smile, "my feelings went away."

Dave Asprey, founder of Bulletproof 360, writes about the fear response:

> By teaching yourself to ignore your fear when there's no reason to be afraid, what you achieve is not courage. It's ignorance. But it's useful ignorance—it lets you temporarily overpower your fear response using sheer will. Since you learned to ignore the feeling of fear, you won't even feel

it when you're using sheer will to overcome that feeling and act anyway.

Using sheer will to overcome irrational fear is a biologically expensive act, and all that wasted energy keeps you from being Bulletproof. When you run out of energy to power your sheer will holding the invisible fear at bay, the fear response from your reptile brain will absolutely interfere with your comprehension, with your focus, and with the way you treat other people. In other words, you'll act like an asshole.

When we are calm in a crisis, whether it is an external crisis or an internal one, we are at a distinct advantage. We are less likely to say things we don't mean and do things we later regret.

Bringing calmness and compassion to your anxious or sad parts is soothing, much like a parent comforting a frightened child. Bringing calm awareness to your triggered parts communicates, "I'm here. I see you. I'm not going anywhere. When you're ready let's talk."

This is what we are all seeking: to be authentically and wholeheartedly accepted in good times and bad and not abandoned. When out of our exhaustion and frustration we attempt to exile critical parts from the younger, more vulnerable parts, we are creating an unhealthy division within ourselves that is tantamount to urban warfare. We are internally splintered. This is harmful and creates chaos leading to more breakdowns. This is when our internal firefighting parts dowse the emotional flames that threaten to overwhelm the individual. Anything can be used as a tranquilizer if we are using it to shut out the truth and hide from ourselves.

We anesthetize ourselves because sensations of trauma are difficult to hold. Of course many people do whatever it takes to extinguish those terrible sensations. The hell with whether they are healthy or not. We are exhausted. We just want to feel better. We just want to be happy.

Supporting Dave Asprey's thoughts on the consequences of being emotionally unhealthy, Dan Harris writes, "When you lurch from one thing to the next, constantly scheming, or reacting to incoming fire, the mind gets exhausted. You get sloppy and make bad decisions."

As we train ourselves to be mindful and grateful, we can anticipate anger or jealousy or panic (even if only a few seconds before we react) and occasionally be able to head them off without saying or doing something we will regret.

A broader and deeper awareness of our sensory experiences and the story we are telling ourselves about those experiences is the essence of remaining calm in a storm. It will prevent unnecessary suffering. Remember, every solution to every impossible problem you will ever face must begin with awareness of its root causes and fears. Sharon Salzberg reminds us with her wise words, "Mindfulness helps us get better at seeing the difference between what's happening and the stories we tell ourselves about what's happening, stories that get in the way of direct experience. Often such stories treat a fleeting state of mind as if it were our entire and permanent self."

14

CURIOSITY VS. ARROGANCE

People who are not curious about themselves, others or life in general are at a distinct disadvantage. They miss opportunities. They lose the chance to meet interesting people. They squander chances to take exciting adventures. The greatest tragedy that befalls these isolated, guarded souls are the adventures that never materialize because they failed to put themselves in destiny's path. History leaves no evidence of the roads not taken.

There is a Zen Buddhist koan that advises, "How a person does one thing is how they do everything." Obviously this is too all-encompassing to be practically relevant all the time, yet it is more true than not true. We should remember this wisdom in regard to others and ourselves. Those who lack a general curiosity toward life will surely not be curious for very long about the unique grooves of your heart, mind and soul.

Being curious requires asking good questions. Learning to ask good questions is an art necessary for achieving extraordinary success. There are perennial stories of curious inventors starting down one path only to be taken far afield from their original idea. This new direction is radically different than where they started yet leads to a new discovery.

Take for example two scientists at the University of Manchester, Andre Geim and Kostya Novoselov. One day while playing around with a piece of graphite and clear adhesive tape attempting to investigate graphite's electrical properties, they made a strange discovery. They needed thinner and thinner pieces of graphite for their work but didn't have a method for achieving this task. What they found by accident was if they dabbed the graphite with tape, it pulled off a thinner layer. The more they repeated the process the smaller they were able to make each layer of graphite. They monitored their progress until they were able to get the material down to their desired one-atom thickness. Graphite at this level coalesces into a new molecular material we now call graphene. It is the strongest material known on planet earth. You will surely be hearing more about this material in years to come. It will revolutionize everything from microchips to mobile phones to radioactive accident cleanup operations like Fukushima.

CURIOSITY VS. ARROGANCE

What does it mean to be curious? It means having a nonjudgmental interest in understanding something or someone. Nonjudgmental. Without judgment. We all have judgmental, hypercritical friends or family members. They are a drag to be around. They complain often and will silently hold you and others in contempt by telegraphing their disdain via body language and/or withholding lighthearted playfulness. These people tend to believe there is a "right" and "wrong" way of doing everything, and of course they are the keepers of the "right" way.

The quality that I have seen most often in those with a lack of curiosity is arrogance. If you will allow me to regress to tenth grade English class for a moment, Merriam-Webster has this to say about arrogance: it is an attitude of superiority manifested in an overbearing manner or in presumptuous claims or assumptions.

Think about it. If you already know the answer, then why ask any questions? If you don't ask questions (or ask them believing you already know the answer), how can you learn anything new? Greek Stoic philosopher Epictetus remarked, "It is impossible for a man to learn what he thinks he already knows." As we will see, confidence in yourself or your idea is not the same thing as arrogance. Confidence is a context-based characteristic grounded in wisdom and experience. Arrogance is a repulsive demonstration of perceived or actual superiority that lacks humility.

Arrogance comes in many forms: entitlement, inflated ego based on wealth, prestigious titles, an inflated ego propped up by physical attractiveness, associates and friends and professional success. Arrogance creeps into a person's words, thoughts and behaviors the way the odor of a dead skunk on a hot Mississippi highway saturates every inch of the unsuspecting cars that pass over the little animal corpse. If you have never experienced this horrid nightmare, consider yourself spared from one less wicked experience.

What, then, are the attributes of a curious person? The curious-minded seeker is constantly searching for new ideas while making interesting connections to other people and experiences where little or no connection existed before (e.g., tape and graphite).

The curious know a secret. They are not discouraged when they try something new and it doesn't work out or leads them down a fruitless rabbit trail. They know for every dead-end path they traverse there will be another trail that will lead them to astounding and profound experiences rife with complexity, beauty and joyful pleasures. Discovering something new is a high that curious people crave.

What does curiosity have to do with solving impossible problems and finding lasting, authentic happiness? Curiosity is the salt that transforms the bland into the interesting. Like a rocket being propelled into space, there are phases to its propulsion systems. The initial boost is to defy the gravitational pull the earth exerts over its physicality. It is a magnificently powerful thrust of energy against gravity. While still tethered to earth's pull, the rocket appears as if it is about to explode. The second stage is still stressful but less violent. It is intended to guide the rocket to its destination. All of the 8 C's are intended to be worked out in stages. Their broad categories parallel the stages of a rocket's propulsion.

The initial internal stage for a person is typically a jarring experience much like the initial stages of a rocket's violent separation from earth. When we are awakened by bad news in the course of everyday life, we are jolted into a new, harsh reality. These moments are usually unanticipated, and therefore we have little time to process them before a response is required. When a situation requires an immediate response, many of us regress to old standbys of fear, attack, withdraw, breakdown.

If the body feels fear but cannot escape its terrifying grip, the sensation will get lodged in the body's memory bank and stored in the unconscious. Any future situation that remotely resembles the trauma will initiate the negative loop. This loop is called chronic stress, which is ground zero for a number of diseases, including heart disease (the number one killer of women in America), high blood pressure and hormone dysregulation, to name just a few.

But what if there were another option than fear? What if there were responses that acknowledged the sensations but did not overwhelm the system with strong negative emotions? Enter compassionate curiosity.

Compassionate curiosity is strong and flexible like graphene. It can bend toward humor and playfulness or be strong and fearless, possessing great courage. In this wide expanse, the potential of curiosity to be healing and restorative is magnified.

When an overwhelming feeling enters our body, we experience it in totality. A natural reaction is to get rid of the negative sensation or the cause of the negative sensation. If the cause of the negative sensation is another person, it is natural to attack them. In attack mode, we are temporarily distracted by our rage or fear. If we do not exercise control over our emotions in this moment, our rational minds turn off. In this state, we often do and say things that we don't fully understand or believe. We say terrible things to those we care about that we later regret and must ask forgiveness. When we return to "normal," we say things like, "I don't know what came over me. It wasn't me. I don't feel that way about you." These events disrupt and often rupture relationships.

But what if instead of lashing out we became curious about our thoughts, our emotions, our bodily sensations with questions like, "Why am I feeling this way *right now*? What part of me is trying to get my attention? What is this part afraid will happen if it doesn't react in this fearful/angry way? What does this part need from me *right now*? How can I take care of this part *right now*? All of these questions stem from a curious mind.

Stealing Fire authors Steven Kotler and Jamie Wheal refer to impossible problems as "wicked problems":

> Solving wicked problems requires more than a direct assault on obvious symptoms [...] The ability to find solutions requires holding conflicting perspectives and using that friction to synthesize a new idea. Developing opposable

mind—a concept developed by Roger Martin of the University of Toronto's Rotman School of Management—isn't easy. If you want to train this kind of creativity and problem solving, what the research shows is that the either/or logic of normal consciousness is simply the wrong tool for the job. The amplified information processing and perspective that non-ordinary states provide can help solve these types of complex problems, and they can often do so faster than more conventional approaches.

What are some of these "non-ordinary states"? These include heart rate variability biofeedback; meditation retreats; attending transformational events like Burning Man; microdosing; sensory deprivation tanks; bodywork such as cranial sacral, Reiki, acupuncture, gyrokinesis; finding flow in your work and relationships; giving radically of your time and resources to your community; committing to a deep spiritual pilgrimage. These are just a few examples.

I often hear clients lament that they feel they do not have any options. "I can't leave my marriage and I can't stay. It will cost too much, and I don't have the money, and it will permanently damage the kids." These are difficult realities to be sure, but they are excuses, not solutions.

Another universal principle we have discussed but is worth repeating is that no matter the situation you always have choices. Always. ALWAYS! It is only through a curious and courageous mind that you can land on the best option. A rash emotional response to a serious situation rarely leads to a thoughtful solution. A lingering procrastination to avoid the hard work of happiness rarely leads to sustainable answers. In my experience, these excuses lead to unnecessary suffering on the path to an eventual solution.

15

COURAGE VS. COWARDICE

All of us will, on occasion, make cowardly decisions at crucial moments out of fear. These fears bully us into emotionally charged, ungrounded, irrational decisions that typically offer short-term benefits but have long-term consequences. Adults avoid suffering like kids recoil from vegetables, homework and cleaning their room. It is instinctual yet counterproductive. If compassion is the castle where the 8 C's dwell, then courage is the king when it comes to taking down impossible problems.

When healthy action is needed but avoided, it inevitably leads to unnecessary suffering. *When healthy action is needed but avoided, it inevitably leads to unnecessary suffering.*

When healthy action is needed but avoided, it inevitably leads to unnecessary suffering.

Here is a cautionary tale when courage was needed but cowardice prevailed. Jon and Cynthia dated for nearly six years. The last three of those years were torturous for both of them. Jon is a soft-spoken, tenderhearted fellow who makes friends easily and goes out of his way to help others. Cynthia is a hard-driving, career-oriented woman who enjoys the finer things in life and manages her "personal brand" meticulously.

They regularly have problems paying their bills on time because of Cynthia's felt need to keep up with the Joneses (either the real Joneses who live next door or the imaginary ones in the media). She has grown intolerant of Jon's lackluster ambition and allows precious few opportunities to pass without letting him feel her rage and disappointment.

Jon's friends beg him to leave Cynthia. However, her paranoia turned abusive when she discovered emails and texts of his friends' opinions of her. She threatened anyone close to him, and as a result, Jon's friends felt the need to protect themselves by setting healthy boundaries with Cynthia, and they stopped reaching out to Jon as often. They were fearful that anything they said might put him in actual physical danger.

Many of Jon's friends had lingering concerns about his well-being. They eventually concocted a cloak-and-dagger system to contact him only at work or when they knew Cynthia was out of town. Jon lives in such fear that he bought a burner, a disposable phone preferred by terrorists and drug dealers, to hide his interactions with friends. He hid it in the deflated spare tire of his car before arriving home each night.

Jon came to see me when he started having suicidal and homicidal thoughts. His first words to me were, "I hope I'm not putting you in any danger." Sensing he was in a crisis, I moved quickly to explain how he has many parts and a *True Self* meant to lead him through these tumultuous times. Jon immediately gravitated to the idea of parts wanting to end his life and the parts that want to end Cynthia's life. He intrinsically understood they were trying to bring him something good and how he wasn't truly suicidal or homicidal. These were simply dramatic metaphors trying to convince him that something needed to be done. He was able to express compassion to each part and how they were extremely polarized from each other.

Jon talked about the parts of him that want to stay with Cynthia. They argued how she wasn't mean all the time as long as she was satisfied by his efforts. This part acknowledged that keeping her satisfied was a Herculean effort with constantly moving goalposts.

The part of Jon that wanted to leave Cynthia was raging mad. It can barely tolerate the parts of him that want to stay and are the origin of his homicidal rage. This part of him cannot fathom life with her. As a result, this part will not give its consent for him to stay in the relationship without making his life a living hell.

Jon was in the midst of a pitched battle both internally and externally. This, he admits, is why he thinks suicide is a reasonable option. His bitter, raging part delivered a message to him in the midst of one of our sessions, "Something or someone has to die here. It's either going to be you, her or the relationship. You choose."

After six months of therapy, Jon came to his session and announced he made a dramatic decision to leave Cynthia for good. There were similar proclamations in the past, and I was uncertain if he would follow through. However, he seemed more resolute than ever.

What made this time different was the letter he wrote Cynthia that he read in our session. It was scathing and personal. It detailed every one of her transgressions over the years. The typed letter was a remarkable twenty-two pages long. He made copies of the letter and gave one to each of his closest friends. He courageously enlisted their support to challenge him if his determination evaporated yet again. He scheduled a "leaving date" on his calendar when he would deliver the letter and move his belongings. His friends banded together and organized a "moving party." He would move out of the house as soon as he handed Cynthia the letter. Several friends anticipated Cynthia becoming violent and paid for an off-duty police officer to assist Jon during the move. They did this as much for their protection as for his.

Three days before it was all set to go down, Jon got the call. It was early Wednesday morning while he was at work. Jon's cell phone buzzed several times. He saw it was Cynthia and ignored her. She texted him, "I'm dying. Literally. Call me when you get a minute."

Jon immediately called his brother who smelled a trap. "She's gone through your stuff again, bro," his brother warned. "Some way, some-how, she knows you're ditching her this weekend. Don't fall for it. Don't call her back. Come over to my house as soon as you get off work."

Jon called Cynthia back against his better judgment. She was not angry. She did not threaten him. She actually sounded like a scared, small child. She was whimpering. In the six years they had been together he had only seen her cry one time.

"Cynthia, what's wrong?" Jon inquired.

"I have Creutzfeldt-Jakob Disease."

After a long pause, "What is that?"

"It's incurable and it's fatal. I don't have a lot of time. The doctors give me six months. Maybe two years."

Jon's mind immediately went to his brother's warning. He was mustering the courage to respond when Cynthia asked him a question, "You won't leave me, will you, Jon? I know I haven't been good to you. I'll change. Please don't leave."

Jon's heart shattered. He knew he would never leave his sick girlfriend no matter how bad she had treated him. He simply couldn't live with himself if he did. "Maybe this was why I was put in her life," he later confided to me.

"Jon?" Cynthia asked in a soft, tender voice he had never heard from her.

"No, Cynthia. I won't leave you."

Jon missed his next therapy appointment. Because of his suicidal and homicidal ideation I reached out. He apologized and set an appointment for later that afternoon.

When Jon arrived he was in tears. He sat on the edge of the couch with his head in his hands. He wept openly with deep sorrow for several long minutes.

"I screwed up. I took too long to make a decision. Now I've got to live with her forever!" he yelled. "I hate her! I hate everything about her."

Jon told me the situation. We explored the idea of her faking an illness, but he said that she is different now. Humbled even. She is not mean nor angry. She is sullen and reflective. Even so, he had to know for himself if she was faking and attended her next doctor's appointment that confirmed without a doubt that she did in fact have the disease.

Jon lamented about the life he had planned for himself. He had befriended a young woman online and was planning a date with her the very weekend of his moving party.

Now his life was over. He couldn't imagine ever being happy again. Jon didn't want to live and wished it were himself that had the disease. He asked forgiveness from me for not acting sooner.

Jon's story is why staying too long in a bad thing is a bad thing that leads to more bad things and prevents good things from happening. Most cases of unnecessary suffering brought on by inaction are not as dramatic as Jon's, yet

COURAGE VS. COWARDICE

many stories I have heard were just as bad. Jon is a chilling reminder of the perils of cowardice.

When we know what to do and don't do it, we are flirting with catastrophe in the form of unnecessary suffering. From a very early age, we learn that life is full of suffering, a lot of which cannot be avoided or even anticipated. It just happens. To add unnecessary suffering is a tragedy.

When we avoid pain in the short term in hopes that the situation will resolve itself, we become the architects of our own suffering. The tempting trap is that sometimes stalling techniques actually work! When the winds of fate do blow in our favor and we make unhealthy choices and avoid suffering, it validates our procrastinatory parts to our own peril. The next time we have an opportunity to put off till tomorrow what could be done today, we are reminded of the few times procrastination worked in our favor. We gamble with the emotional lottery and hope against hope that maybe what worked before will work again. We hope to postpone difficult conversations or maybe not have to have them at all.

Another trap we rationalize away is that often the painful consequences we suffer are not as painful as we had imagined. When this occurs, it further reinforces the bad habit of avoidance. We muddle through and eventually feel good about our resiliency. That is until another unforeseen, unpredictable catastrophe blows up in our face, and we once again lament our terrible fate.

Jon rolled the dice by not taking action sooner with Cynthia and lost. It is good to remember in situations like Jon's that life, the Universe, God, whatever you want to call it plays by her own rules. Play with fire long enough and you are bound to get burned. Jon will never know what paths may have opened up for him if he had acted with courage.

Make a pact between your *True Self* and all of your parts that starting today you will begin to face your deepest fears as they arise. Even small decisions like buying a book on a topic you are struggling with or watching an inspirational TED Talk or attending your first Alcoholics/Narcotics/Sexaholics Anonymous meeting are steps toward a liberated mind and a happy life. Remind yourself that even one good decision is progress. Stacking many good decisions is a sure path to lasting happiness.

What does courage look like in the face of fear? Fears are like Legos. At first they appear as innocuous little pieces randomly scattered around your house. That is until you step on them in the middle of the night. But the more you pick them up and inspect them, you begin to realize they fit together to form bigger fears. Before you know it, you are surrounded by enormous fear structures that feel overwhelming. How do you face your fears? You begin addressing each fear, one at a time, as they arise.

As you bring compassion to the parts of you that are struggling with fear, real and/or imagined, you will begin to feel calmer. As your system settles down, you can then be curious about why certain parts are triggered and what those parts need.

It is obvious why courage is necessary when facing impossible problems. Much of what drives our cowardly fears will never happen. Those things we fear that are likely to happen are manageable. Those truly big monsters under our bed at night that could happen (e.g., our marriage ending, financial bankruptcy, death) are truly colossal and should be given due respect. But it is unhealthy to mix up these categories, and that is exactly what we do all the time. We mix up what will most likely never happen and is not that important with things that could happen and are truly important. This is a serious error.

It takes courage to leap off the side of a cliff wearing nothing more than a wing suit. It takes courage to confront your accuser in court. It takes courage to fight against injustice and evil knowing that neither of those forces plays fair. It takes courage to own your fears, face your fears and take action in the face of what you fear the most. That is what impossible problems are: a gift box full of fear offering you an opportunity to grow up a little bit more. Courage is the mental and moral toughness necessary to tackle danger, fear or difficulty. In his autobiography *Undisputed Truth*, Mike Tyson writes about the wisdom his beloved trainer Cus D'Amato shared with him about courage:

> You think you know the difference between a hero and a coward, Mike? Well, there is no difference between a hero and a coward in what they feel. It's what they do that makes them different. The hero and the coward feel exactly the same but you have to have the discipline to do what a hero does and to keep yourself from doing what the coward does.

16

CONNECTED VS. LONELY

Our desperate attempts to escape the prison of loneliness and feel deeply connected to others can, at times, usurp even our most basic instincts of self-preservation.

Gail Maeder was barely 22 years old when she left her hometown of Sag Harbor in 1992. Her petite frame and innocent eyes revealed a naivety that made her instantly approachable. Yet it was her affable approachability that often made others uneasy for her safety. They instinctually felt the qualities that made her so demure and deferential could, in the wrong hands, put her in danger. Evidence of her loving, trusting nature could be seen in how much she cared for animals. Her desire to do good and be good surfaced in her mildly irrational refusal to use paper towels on the moral belief that paper towels contributed to the murder of trees.

In a 1997 *New York Times*[1] article, Gail's parents talked of when she first moved to California. She eked out a meager but happy existence with her boyfriend doing odd jobs to make ends meet. She opened a small shop and cleaned houses to pay the rent. However, it didn't take long before her life started to unravel.

One domino of bad luck fell, then another. First she and her boyfriend broke up. Without his help she could not pay her bills. Her tenuous financial situation resulted in losing her business. The pressures of financial hardship and a persistent melancholy from the breakup pulled her into a dark depression. It was in this vulnerable, lonely state she first heard of Heaven's Gate. The group met near her home, and one evening when she hesitantly attended one of their classes, they, like so many others, received her with open arms.

Her parents first heard of her involvement with this cult when she sent them a note scrawled on the back of one of their flyers. The message was simple and straightforward, "This is what I'm doing. Don't worry. I'm happy." And she was.

Video and audio recordings of Gail during this time show a strong-willed woman able to resist the desperate pleadings of her frightened parents' begging her to return home. Her parents were so alarmed they started recording the few

---

1 http://www.nytimes.com/1997/03/30/us/time-of-puzzled-heartbreak-binds-relatives.html

conversations they were able to have with her. They tried unsuccessfully to lure her home for a visit, thinking they could whisk her away for therapy and reprogramming. But Gail remained polite yet firm. During these phone conversations she giggled uncomfortably, avoiding the sensitive topic of her having joined a cult. Her message to her parents was clear and unwavering: No, Mom and Dad, I'm not coming home. And she never did.

The last video taken before the group's now infamous mass suicide is eerily peaceful. Each person is achingly happy about the prospect of being taken as a "class" by aliens whose spaceship is hiding in the tail of the Hale-Bopp Comet. Gail has an expression of what appears to be delight, but she looks gaunt and malnourished. Her shaved head and sunken cheeks are reminiscent of Holocaust survivors. She looks decades older than her chronological age and is barely recognizable from the photos taken in Sag Harbor just a few years before.

On March 19, 1997, 39 members of the Heaven's Gate cult began taking a mixture of phenobarbital, alcohol and hydrocodone mixed with applesauce or pudding. Leaving nothing to chance, each member tied a plastic bag around their heads to induce asphyxiation.

Gail's story represents an extreme version of the desire to belong. Most of us will never join a cult. However, might our loneliness be causing us to stay in an unhealthy relationship too long? Pick up people at bars for casual sex not knowing if they are good, trustworthy individuals? Keep friends around who do not build us up and help us become better versions of ourselves?

In March 2017, the *Boston Globe*[2] published an article titled, "The Biggest Threat To Middle-Aged Men Isn't Smoking Or Obesity. It's Loneliness." In his article, Billy Baker discussed how easy it is for men to slip into the routine of work, home, work, home, work, home.

Baker writes:

> Beginning in the 1980's, (researcher Richard) Schwartz says, study after study started showing that those who were more socially isolated were much more likely to die during a given period than their socially connected neighbors, even after you corrected for age, gender, and lifestyle choices like exercising and eating right. Loneliness has been linked to an increased risk of cardiovascular disease and stroke and the progression of Alzheimer's. One study found that it can be as much of a long-term risk factor as smoking.

Being connected to others is not simply a nice emotional pick-me-up. It is a biological imperative. If isolation and loneliness are the hallmarks of an emotionally unhealthy individual, what does connectedness look like, and how can it help you solve your impossible problems and find lasting, authentic happiness?

One of my favorite moments with a client is when they first come to understand the multiplicity of their minds.

---

2 https://www.bostonglobe.com/magazine/2017/03/09/the-biggest-threat-facing-middle-age-men-isn-smoking-obesity-loneliness/k6saC9FnnHQCUbf5mJ8okL/story.html

I know the benefits they will reap by integrating the idea that they are not one monolithic personality but rather are composed of a vast array of unique parts as well as a *True Self*. I get excited as I watch them make the leap to understanding how their minds are constructed. They describe how this new idea feels intuitively right as if they knew it all along but had yet to actually name it.

This new framework explains why for so long they have felt the cognitive dissonance of one part wanting one thing and another part wanting another. While stress feels uncomfortable in the body, being able to understand that only part of you is unhappy allows you to focus your attention on a specific part or parts. This unique way of thinking about one's self offers practical remedies to this cognitive dissonance dilemma.

Prior to this radical shift in perspective, clients struggled to reconcile parts with wildly differing beliefs on the same subject. Rather than fearing they must be losing their mind with all the voices in their head, they now say with confidence, "Part of me feels X, but another part of me feels Y and that's okay."

Connecting with each individual part, understanding its needs, hearing its stories and tending to its wounds are all vital ingredients for a healthy mental operating system. It is the same thing with a family, organization or corporation. If the members of a group don't have confidence in their leader or feel valued and their problems understood, they will do one of two things: leave or protest.

A person can protest or leave in many ways. An employee can quit, or they can stay and sabotage the organization. A child can protest by isolating themselves in their room, refusing to participate in family activities. Our internal parts are no different than an employee or child. They can isolate themselves and hide their emotions deep in the psyche, or they can erupt into our lives through erratic behaviors like drunkenness, anxiety or fear. If they are hiding, it is because they feel hurt or scared. If they are protesting, it is because they feel dismissed. They are trying to tell you something they believe is important.

Connectedness embeds a deep richness and grounded resilience to life. We all want to know who has our backs when things get hard. It is just as rewarding to know who we can call at 3:00 A.M. as it is for someone to know they can call us.

Billy Baker was appalled when asked to write an article about middle-aged men who don't have friends. He was certain he was not the loneliest man on earth as his editor suggested. Baker writes:

> There were all those other good friends who feel as if they're still in my lives because we keep tabs on one another via social media, but as I ran down the list of those I'd consider real, true, life-long friends, I realized that it had been years since I'd seen many of them, even decades for a few.
>
> By the time I got back to my desk, I realized that I was indeed perfect for this story, not because I

was unusual in any way, but because my story is very, very typical. And as I looked into what that means, I realized that in the long term, I was heading down a path that was very, very dangerous.

Connectedness takes intentional effort. Isolation takes little to no action. It is relatively easy to drift away from relationships with nothing more than a passing thought, convincing ourselves, "I'll get together with [X] next time" or "I'll call [Y] tomorrow."

There are no silver bullets when solving life's impossible problems, but there are a few habits that can make solving them easier (or more difficult). Stacking one good decision on top of another is a good example of a habit that will increase your odds of solving life's daunting problems. Not only do these and other healthy strategies create a resilient mind, they inculcate positive habits that help prevent future problems from occurring. Getting and staying connected to others opens you up to new ways of thinking and resources that you could not know on your own. Gail is an example of our deep need for connection and our willingness to sacrifice even our own health and safety to belong.

For some, getting and staying connected is as natural as breathing. For others, however, it requires heroic feats to overcome the siege of unconscious resistance. Introverts and those with avoidant attachment styles tend toward solitude and solitary activities. They naturally prefer to avoid events that zap their vitality.

Those who are avoidant and/or introverted must respect the protests their internal parts are registering. If they do not, they risk alienating those parts and potentially instigating a mutiny.

While many parts want to isolate, especially during times of challenge or exhaustion, being clued in to those parts that need support, help, guidance offers them a platform to speak for their needs. Our internal worlds are complex and adaptable. Often our parts just need to be acknowledged for them to let go of their protest. They do not expect to be catered to *every time* they have a need, but they do expect to be respected enough to be heard. Sometimes they just need to vent…just like you and I.

As a culture, we have fashioned institutions to keep us connected: Religion. Sports. Fraternities. Sororities. Country clubs. Political parties. Book clubs. Bars. Facebook. Instagram. Cults. These and countless other opportunities are all around us. Yet we can mindlessly engage in any of these meaningful institutions without reaping their intended benefits. One important question to ask yourself is, "How deeply connected am I to the individuals in the various groups where I spend my time and money?"

People who have attended the same church for years may be less connected to others in their congregation than a neighborhood book club that has only been meeting for a few weeks but are engaging in deep, thoughtful conversations. An important factor for connectedness with yourself and others is not duration of time but the quality of the time spent. Length of time is nearly irrelevant.

Anyone with a dysfunctional, disconnected family understands this all too well!

The good news is that the same way you get connected to others is the same way you get connected to your internal parts. You make time for them. You ask them good questions. You care for them in times of need. You celebrate them with gratitude and joy during good times. Sometimes it requires nothing more than listening as Rachel Naomi Remen beautifully observes, "The most basic and powerful way to connect with another person is to listen. Just listen. Perhaps the most important thing we ever give each other is our attention...a loving silence often has far more power to heal and to connect than the most well-intentioned words."

17

CREATIVITY VS. RIGIDITY

When faced with a challenging life situation, we all instinctively reach into our tried-and-true bag of tricks, no matter how healthy or unhealthy they may be, to fix the problem. It has taken us a lifetime to collect these doohickeys and thingamajigs. "If it worked once," we wager, "it's bound to work again." This works most of the time with the majority of our problems. But what happens when none of our tools work?

Inevitably we return to our toolbox again and again, convinced we have overlooked just the right tool. More time passes, and a slow dawning emerges that maybe we don't have the skills necessary to solve our dilemma. In our desperation, we seek the solace and support of romantic partners, close friends and maybe a few trusted family members. If those fail to provide us with adequate solutions, we move to our third-string problem-solving crew such as our hairdresser, family physician and The Google. If all these fail, we resort to bargaining with God and finally psychotherapy.

Thankfully, most of our problems are resolved quickly. However, some defy attempts at easy, straightforward solutions. The sin many of us commit when our go-tos don't work is that we fail to put on our thinking caps and look for creative solutions. Even though scientists now know our brains possess the wonderful ability to adapt, called "plasticity," changing patterns of thinking and acting is beyond difficult.

The more we repeat habits, the more likely we are to repeat those habits. Another obstacle to changing unhealthy habits is how we often mindlessly repeat what we already know doesn't work. This autopilot behavior is responsible for much of our unnecessary suffering.

Changing unhealthy habits takes willpower and creativity. Pulitzer Prize–winning journalist Charles Duhigg writes in *The Power of Habit: Why We Do What We Do In Life And Business*:

> Once you know (an unhealthy) habit exists, you have the responsibility to change it...others have done so. Perhaps a sleep-walking murderer can plausibly argue that he wasn't aware of his habit, and so he doesn't bear responsibility for his crime,

CREATIVITY VS. RIGIDITY

but almost all of the other patterns that exist in most people's lives — how we eat and sleep and talk to our kids, how we unthinkingly spend our time, attention and money — those are habits that we know exist. And once you understand that habits can change, you have the freedom and the responsibility to remake them. Once you understand that habits can be rebuilt, the power of habit becomes easier to grasp and the only option left is to get to work...Change might not be fast and it isn't always easy. But with time and effort, almost any habit can be reshaped.

Being creative, like being happy, is good, fun, hard work. Creative problem solvers initially see a problem just like the rest of us. They too want to be efficient with their time and energy and reach into their bag of tricks in an effort to solve the problem in the shortest possible time. However, when those tricks don't work, they don't keep trying the same key that didn't unlock the door five seconds ago. They quickly move on.

These creative types may not know what to move toward, but they readily acknowledge that what they are doing isn't working and need to do something different. This rapid movement toward accepting/embracing/experimenting is a hallmark trait of creativity. It differentiates people who are successful in love and life from the herd.

If you want to boost your creative energy, start by exercising. Duhigg continues, "Typically, people who exercise start eating better and become more productive at work. They smoke less and show more patience with colleagues and family. They use their credit cards less frequently and say they feel less stressed. Exercise is a keystone habit that triggers widespread change."

Carol Dweck is one of the leading researchers in the field of motivation, personality and development. She opens her 2014 TED Talk[1] with a brief story of creativity in education:

> I heard about a high school in Chicago where students had to pass a certain number of courses to graduate, and if they didn't pass a course, they got the grade 'Not Yet.' And I thought that was fantastic, because if you get a failing grade, you think, I'm nothing, I'm nowhere. But if you get the grade 'Not Yet,' you understand that you're on a learning curve. It gives you a path into the future.

Dweck's creative research led her to discover two very different perceptual frameworks that occur when a person is confronted with a challenging experience.

The first mindset refers to people who believe success is derived from innate talent or ability given from birth. This "fixed" mindset, as Dweck refers to it, theorizes that a person's intelligence and basic abilities are fixed traits that have an upper limit no matter how much effort one expends. The second mindset believes that success is based primarily on effort, hard work, learning new skills and the grittiness of perseverance. This is referred to as a "growth" mindset.

---

[1] https://www.ted.com/talks/carol_dweck_the_power_of_believing_that_you_can_improve/transcript?language=en#t-28615

CREATIVITY VS. RIGIDITY

To understand which mindset you possess, take an unvarnished, courageous look at your thoughts and behaviors over some of your most recent (big or small) relational, personal or professional flops. How did you handle failure/rejection/disappointment? Did you continue working hard to solve the problem despite setbacks and failures? Those who possess a growth mindset don't see the obstacles in their way as insurmountable. They believe they have simply "not yet" found a solution.

Dweck believes wholeheartedly that a person can change their mindset from fixed to growth. On her website,[2] she outlines four steps to changing one's mindset:

Step 1: Learn how to hear your fixed mindset "voice"

Step 2: Recognize that you have a choice

Step 3: Talk back to the fixed mindset voice with a growth mindset voice

Step 4: Take the growth mindset action (face challenges enthusiastically, learn from setbacks, listen to criticism)

Creatively solving impossible problems relies heavily on the growth mindset. Repeating the same unhealthy behaviors and hoping for a different result is a fixed mindset and Einstein's definition of insanity.

Our parts are independent subpersonalities each with their own wishes, hopes, fears and motivations. It would

---

2 https://mindsetonline.com/changeyourmindset/firststeps/index.html

logically follow then that some parts possess a growth mindset while others have a fixed mindset.

The parts of you that are healthy are more likely to possess a growth mindset. Through luck, love and/or hard work, these parts have successfully navigated around the hazards that threaten their sanity.

Healthy parts only need attention and occasional guidance from your *True Self*. They can work autonomously for the most part. The most bang for your buck then comes from working with the parts that are stuck in the past reliving old wounds.

When a part is stuck reliving the past, two unfortunate things happen: A) The part perpetually repeats the thoughts and behaviors that were formed during the wounding experience, and B) the part protests fearfully in frantic attempts to avoid ever being hurt in the same or similar way again.

A wounded part lives in the immediacy of now yet ironically not really present to the now. It has only short-term benefits in mind, such as, "How can I escape this pain *right now!*" This is the problem parts have of being blinded by the tyranny of now. They only see their pain as negative, not as a potential path to healing and thriving.

A part with a growth mindset realizes that sometimes suffering is unavoidable, loss is a part of life and endings are inevitable. This part isn't fearful of pain and suffering. It finds ways to use it to gain greater insight. It loathes the idea of wasting a perfectly good opportunity for self-reflection and growth.

CREATIVITY VS. RIGIDITY

Without creativity you cannot solve your impossible problems. Rigidity of thinking will hamper your ability to adapt to change and, less likely, to hold onto any gains you make toward solving your problems.

One of my clients uses the metaphor of an enchanted forest to navigate her internal world. Actions in the real world affect her enchanted forest. Another client uses active imagination, a tool utilized by Carl Jung and Robert Johnson, to tap the unconscious world with imagination. Another client draws her parts as little children. Another client tells the stories of her parts through her writing. All of these people are weaving and expressing their internal and external worlds together with imagination.

For example, it may be more helpful for an alcoholic to analogize her addiction as a three-headed dragon than a bottle hidden in the garage. Using her imagination to fight the dragon of addiction in her mind is a step in the direction of dealing with the flask tucked away in her purse. What does it matter how she gets to healthy as long as she is continually moving in that direction?

Creativity persists despite setbacks and failures because there will always be setbacks and failures. It will rain on your wedding day. You will lose your job in an up market. You will break a leg on a skiing trip to Aspen. Setbacks are inevitable. Fight like hell to avoid impossible problems, but fight like hell when they come too. They are gift boxes full of shit wrapped in barbed wire. Seeing the inherent value through creative eyes with a growth mindset makes your success inevitable.

18

CONFIDENCE VS. INSECURITY

In 2005 Rosa Parks was the first woman and only the second African American to lie in state in the Capitol Rotunda in Washington, D. C., for her courageous acts of heroism. One hundred seven years earlier, the woman who served as one of the inspirations for Mrs. Parks', revolutionary act, Mrs. Septima Clark, was born into a conflicted and repressive world for African Americans in the highly segregated city of Charleston, South Carolina.

Parks had this to say about Mrs. Clark:

> I am always very respectful and very much in awe of the presence of Septima Clark, because her life

story makes the effort that I have made very minute. I only hope that there is a possible chance that some of her great courage and dignity and wisdom has rubbed off on me.

Mrs. Clark had no photographers snapping pictures of her as she made her declarations of freedom in an oppressed community. There were no cameras rolling capturing her dramatic, persistent resistance. Martin Luther King Jr. never took up her cause. She did her work for the most part in obscurity. As a child, even her own home was not safe from her mother's tyranny of segregation. Her mother held her daughters to a harsher standard than her sons.

Mrs. Clark's father was a slave on John Poinsette's plantation. Poinsette was a prominent Charleston politician who also became the namesake to the perennial Christmas decoration—the poinsettia plant.

Mrs. Clark's mother yearned to belong to the middle-class society but was never able to transition beyond her working-class status.

At six years old, Mrs. Clark was removed from a school that housed more than a hundred black students who spent their days sitting outside on the steps learning nothing. Her mother convinced an elderly woman who lived across the street from the school to teach her girls how to read and write.

At that time there were no high schools for black children in Charleston. Yet throughout her life, Clark would not only graduate from college but also receive her bachelor's from Benedict College and a master's degree from

Hampton University. Later in life she established the Citizenship Schools where she taught illiterate adults to read throughout the Deep South.

Septima Clark had a few impossible problems of her own. Her father was a slave forced to serve as a messenger for the Confederate troops. Her mother was tortured with envy that eventually drove a wedge between mother and daughter, all for the purpose of social class elevation that never materialized. Five years after getting married, Mrs. Clark's husband died. Clark lost her job as a teacher when she refused to renounce the NAACP. As a public employee, this act of attrition was illegal. In 1965 Mrs. Clark wrote, "The greatest evil in our country today is not racism, but ignorance."

If courage is something Septima Clark had, confidence is something she felt that motivated her actions. We can, and often do, fake what other people see compared to what we feel. However, what others cannot see and what we cannot easily hide from ourselves is how confident we feel. Confidence is something you feel. You don't have to drum it up with positive affirmations. Confidence is the innate belief that we have what we need to solve our own problems no matter how powerful the adversary or how much the odds are stacked against us. It isn't the belief that you will win no matter what—that is dangerous, inflated arrogance. But it is the confidence that you have what it takes and if you give it your best effort and get a little lucky along the way, you might succeed. As the great scientist Louis Pasteur noted, "Fortune favors the prepared mind."

Victory over impossible problems favors those who spend the extra hours studying, reading and training.

The first draft of this chapter ended above. As I edited the book over and over, it dawned on me that the chapter on confidence was only two pages long. I pondered this for a while before realizing that of all the 8 C's I was least confident in Confidence.

I found this distressing, but it wasn't a new revelation to me. This dynamic has played out in my personal and professional life in big and small ways. However, as if on cue, my courageous, creative and compassionate parts rushed to the challenge, seeking solutions to this impossible problem of mine. I sensed that my perennial struggle with confidence might somehow be beneficial in serving the purposes of this book of helping others confront their fears and solve their impossible problems.

More than anyone, I am eager to turn my obstacle into an opportunity. To do so it is imperative I change my mindset from, "I am not a confident person" to "How can I learn to be more confident?" If, as Ryan Holiday says, the obstacle is the way, then how is having less confidence than I desire the way forward for me right now?

My first act was to own that this is an area where I can grow. My creative part suggested that while there may be instances when I need to "fake it till I make it," this was not one of them. I had more to gain by acknowledging I am not an expert on confidence than by bluffing. Next was to extend compassion and courage to the parts of me that feel scared and insecure. I let go of the expectation that every part of me has to be an expert on every one of the 8 C's before I could publish a book, give a lecture or teach a workshop on them. By confidently embracing my lack of confidence and still taking action to write this book, I was not letting my lack of confidence hold me back.

After realizing that my obstacle could be a way forward, I embraced curiosity by asking people who knew me well to share with me their opinion of my confidence. I asked people who I thought were confident their view on the matter. I also sat quietly and engaged in thoughtful reflection. This exercise revealed that I might be more confident in myself and my abilities than I initially gave myself credit for. I created fantasy dialogues with friends and others and imagined what they might say to the question, "What is confidence?" And of course I Googled confidence and found a host of interesting articles.

In my pursuit of understanding my relationship with confidence, I examined factors responsible for confidence in children from parenting to genetics. I also thought about confidence in terms of the Enneagram, Adult Attachment and Internal Family Systems. I realized that my avoidant attachment style to others is based on an unstable (insecure) foundation. Remember there are three main types of attachment: secure, anxious and avoidant. What the research suggests is that anxious and avoidant both originate from the same base of insecurity. Research shows two important factors supporting this. First, the children with avoidant attachment showed the same disrupted biological responses but did not outwardly manifest these symptoms. That means the avoidant child feels anxious but shows stoicism. Second, when an avoidant person becomes emotionally ungrounded, they begin to act like an anxiously attached individual. What this points to is a partial biological basis for my feelings of lack of confidence. I then began to think about my high sexual (one-to-one bonding) instinct regarding my Enneagram personality type. If I am most comfortable in intimate one-on-one conversations, then I would certainly feel less confident when speaking to a larger group of people or socializing in a crowd. This was another clue to why I may feel, but not necessarily be, less confident.

What, then, is confidence? Confidence is the assurance or belief in a plan, purpose or action. How does this characteristic look in real life? Here are a few thoughts:

- Confident people take risks in business and relationships. Leaders know the power of a confident persona and don't share their fears and concerns with those who have no power to change or help the situation.

- Confident people are willing to fail because they don't see most failure at a task as a negative reflection on their personal character. It is simply an opportunity to learn something new. They believe they possess what they already need to be successful: hard work, tenacity, humility and intelligence.

- Confident people are willing to respectfully disappoint others and not let the other person's reactions negatively impact their mood.

- Confident people are present to the moment. If they are

nervous, they name it. If they are happy, they name it. They own what they feel without shame.

- Confident people don't catastrophize about every bad thing that *could* happen. They believe they have the capacity to handle whatever situation comes their way. If they get in over their heads, they are absolutely fine with asking for help.

- Confident people believe in their abilities before there is evidence to prove it.

- Confident people are willing to bluff in a situation because they understand bluffing, which is different than lying, will embolden others and increase their chances of success. Bluffing is being willing to take action before having 100 percent assurance of succeeding.

Second, while I have a strong grasp of the seven other C's, there may be those who struggle with some of the other "C" words. What could my struggle with being confident teach them about what to do if they feel deficient in one or more of the 8 C's?

On a recent beach vacation I lost my sunglasses. Having paid a hefty sum for them, I was not pleased. I had them for upwards of four years, which is a record for me. I felt I had gotten my money's worth, but I was still not happy. When buying my previous pair, I purchased eight pairs of glasses (and returned seven) before finding just the right pair.

There is one thing you need to know about me: I have a square head. It's like a block of wood with ears, eyes, nose, mouth and hair. I was well into my thirties before I learned to tame my hair in such a way that didn't automatically give away my squarehead status. I also have what some call a "weak" chin and moderately wide jowls. There are bigger jowls out there to be sure, but mine are by no means small. Why am I telling you this? Because the shape of the head and face dramatically impacts how sunglasses look on a person's face.

I walked into Sunglass Universe and shared with the salesperson the sob story about losing my sunglasses. I tell her what I am looking for, and she directs me to a bay of elegantly lit glass cabinets. She hands me a pair, and I mention my squareheadedness, and before I could barely finish my sentence, the sales rep accosted me, "Stop with the complaining. People come in here all day with their insecurities."

I was taken aback by her strong opinions and decided to continue shopping without responding. I continued, "The shape of my head determines the type of glasses..." She cut me off again, "You are fine just the way you are. We all are."

I realized that this sales representative was processing her own issues and that it wasn't about me. What I said next though surprised and delighted me, "I don't have a problem with insecurity. I kind of like myself. A lot." She turned to look at me, probing for sarcasm. When she didn't find any, she responded, "Huh. Good."

I share this story because it isn't every day that we get to overtly express our confidence with ourselves. Most of the time, confidence is surreptitiously tested through indirect means or challenges by others. I was pleased that when caught off guard by the abrupt comments of the sales rep that I leapt to my own defense. It seems there are some parts of me that are very confident and very happy with who I am and who I have become.

19

CLARITY VS. CONFUSION

Recently I was in a session with a relatively new client named Carrie. She was distraught to learn she was a Type 2 on the Enneagram. This type is overly concerned with being a supportive, caring helper to others. She was a little "creeped out" at how accurate the test and the lengthy description were in revealing her most inner thoughts and private behaviors.

Carrie resonated deeply when she discovered that one of the greatest gifts of a Type 2 is to be of service to others. However, what unsettled her most was to learn how manipulative Type 2s can be when they are unhealthy. They will serve others in order to get their needs met. When that fails, and it fails often, it leads to anger and resentment, yet they rarely express their disappointment. Unhealthy Type 2s are not in touch with their needs and loathe confrontation as it disrupts the social contract of niceness. It is as if the manipulative behavior begets the resentment, which then restarts the manipulative loop. Inevitably this leads to exhaustion and an emotional breakdown. This breakdown could turn into an actual emotional outburst. It could also go underground, resulting in depression or anxiety. The worst part for Carrie was to realize that she has engaged in this manipulative behavior many times without realizing what she was doing.

Carrie also identified her attachment style. She immediately recognized her anxious attachment to others. She acknowledged how her adult son, who still lived with her at home, was often the target of her manipulative behaviors. Carrie never married his father. When he left the relationship, he told her there were two problems he couldn't deal with. The first, he said, was how he felt controlled. The second reason, he told her, was because she was too needy. He felt like if he went anywhere or did anything, she was always checking up on him. At the time his reasons broke her heart. Her friends told her that he didn't know what a good thing he was missing and encouraged her to dismiss his complaints as a man who didn't know what he wanted.

Now, however, Carrie has a deeper understanding of how she would manipulate him with little gifts or acts of kindness. She convinced herself this is what he would like because that's what she wanted him to do for her. That is not what he wanted. Just as important, Carrie was able to recognize that she would always get anxious when he left with friends or had an overnight business trip. She chalked it up to her intuition and scanned every detail upon his return. She sniffed the collars of his shirts and monitored their bank account for any out-of-the-ordinary cash withdrawals around the time of his trips. She did this because she was scared he might be having an affair or paying for prostitutes though there was no evidence whatsoever to substantiate those claims.

Now she realizes, as someone who has an anxious attachment to others, that she was living out her unconscious attachment fears through her suspicious, paranoid behaviors. Her relentless calls demanding to know where he was and who he was with are what ended their relationship.

As Carrie gained greater self-awareness, the qualities that she once considered "just who I am" were in fact changeable. She started to notice in the moment when she was being manipulative to get her needs met. With this awareness, she then worked hard to determine what her needs were and ask for what she needed. If the person could not or would not meet her needs, then she would need to ask herself hard questions of whether or not this was a healthy relationship for her.

Carrie also understood that no one in a romantic relationship wanted to feel as if they were being tracked. She intuitively knew that her anxious attachment had killed more than one relationship in the past. She was determined to not let it take down another one.

"Before I learned about my Enneagram type and attachment style," she confided to me at the end of one of her sessions, "I felt as if I were like a seed being blown around by the wind without any direction. I was vulnerable to even the slightest gust. I got whipped around a lot, and I didn't know why. I had no idea that I actually have a choice in the matter. I just thought this is who I am and I'm never going to change." We both sat with her seed analogy for a few moments. I began to have a dawning realization of the brilliance of her analogy.

"Carrie," I said with a building enthusiasm, "I think you are on to something. When I meet new clients, I know in a short period of time their personality and attachment style. But I encounter resistance because of what you just described. Most people think they are who they are. They don't understand how much influence they can exert on the unconscious network of personality, attachment style or their many parts. When they wake up to their potential, they are able to radically change their life for the better."

I paused for a moment to gather my thoughts before continuing.

"It is as if we are all seeds, and the wind is the randomness of life. It just whips us around with seemingly little care. But inside each of us is this great intelligence in the form of our majestic minds. This organ houses our personality, attachment style and all of our many parts. When a seed is given the right conditions of light, water, soil and a certain amount of stress, it grows and becomes stronger. In the same way, an individual will thrive in a healthy environment. They become the best version of what they were intended to be. Conversely, if a seed falls on asphalt, it will just wither away. This is the person who never understands or never has the opportunities to appreciate who they are and the great potential buried within them. There is a deep intelligence inherent in all of us waiting to flourish."

Carrie was able to capture a first glimpse of clarity into her essence through her diligent efforts studying the Enneagram, learning her attachment style and investigating her parts and *True Self*.

Clarity is the result of facing fears and courageously confronting impossible problems. The 8 C's of *compassion, courage, calm, curiosity, creativity, connectedness, confidence* will always serve as a perpetual guide into greater *clarity*.

As would be expected, the antithesis of the 8 C's of *apathy, chaos, arrogance, loneliness, rigidity, cowardice and insecurity* are a rickety stairwell descending into *confusion*.

Each and every word in this book is intended to provide greater clarity and lift the veil of confusion about who you are, what to do with your impossible problems and how to find lasting, authentic happiness. I want you to have clarity around why you do what you do and how you can most benefit yourself and others.

When it gets down to it, so much of what we do is to gain clarity. It isn't so much that we don't have the courage to act when needed. Most of us when we know the right thing to do can muster the grit and determination to make it happen. The problem arises when confusion sets in about what needs to be done.

Impossible problems are rarely, if ever, black and white affairs. They are wrought with conflicting and often confounding variables that negate one another's relevance. What, then, do you do when clarity is elusive?

Socrates said, "The secret of change is to focus all your energy, not fighting the old, but building the new."

Like money, clarity cannot be pursued directly (unless you are a bank robber). It is an effect, not a cause. I have come to believe that we never exist in a neutral state in regard to our physical, emotional or spiritual health. We are either progressing in the direction of health or regressing backwards into unhealthiness. Sometimes the progress or regression is almost imperceptibly subtle. Other times our rise or fall is dramatic. In all of it I have never witnessed a neutral state. Even the smallest of actions, like making your bed, flossing every day, making eye contact with the kids and giving them a hug and a kiss before walking out the door, are important steps in the direction of health. In the same way, little indiscretions serve as warning beacons flashing in the dark, indicating a lack of integrity, wisdom and mindfulness.

We must make it a habit to extend ourselves compassion when, from time to time, we come up short of our own expectations. In those moments what matters most is how quickly we regain our footing and make amends for our less than stellar moments. There is a Japanese proverb that says, "Fall down seven; get up eight." Extending ourselves grace is a realignment of values that rights our ship and once again moves us closer to our goals. This is not weakness. It is, in fact, the exact opposite and the quickest path back to health and happiness. When we mentally abuse ourselves, we perpetuate the attempts of those who tried to destroy us in the past. This is a tragic but all too common example of unnecessary suffering.

20

CLARITY

The Art of Deep Listening

One would think writing a chapter on clarity given all the words that have come before would be easy. However, I found the opposite to be true. Ironically, I found clarity to be elusive.

I knew I wanted a summary of how the other 8 C's work together to bring clarity to an impossible problem. Yet I couldn't find the right collection of ideas to capture that message. Then came the "seed" conversation with my client. It felt good to share this client's epiphany, but when I finished writing it, I sensed there was more to say, yet I couldn't formulate my ideas. I decided to extend myself some grace and give myself a break from writing. Two weeks later I was still confused.

Then, out of nowhere my A-ha! Moment came rushing to my mind, "Isn't there research describing how flashes of inspiration often happen in the shower?" I Googled it and there it was. That article led to other research studies, and before I knew it the chapter had written itself.

These flashes of inspiration are called by many names: Eureka Moments, A-ha! Moments, Sudden Insights, Epiphanies, etc. They are critical to solving impossible problems. But first we must understand how our brain works in its *Default Mode*.

The Default Mode Network (DMN) is a relatively new discovery. The basic idea of DMN is that when our minds are at rest, there is a certain type of activity that continues to happen in specific regions of the brain. The idea of our brains still being active even when we are not engaged in a focused activity began in the 1930s through the research of Hans Berger. Fast-forward forty years, and David Ingvar showed a particular pattern of blood flow in the brains of many research participants while they were unfocused and at ease.

Advances in neuroimaging gave rise to more accurate testing and data collection. During the early 2000s, researchers from Washington University and others began publishing studies clearly showing areas of the brain most active while at rest. In these articles one of the researchers called the resting state of research participants the *Default Mode*. The name caught on, and the grouping of brain regions active during the *Default Mode* became known as the *Default Mode Network*.

There is a famous story of these sudden flashes of inspiration that has been around for centuries. It involves a Roman writer, a king, a naked mathematician and a man's life hanging in the balance.

The naked mathematician was Archimedes, and the author, architect and engineer was Vitruvius. In the introduction to his ninth volume of *De architectura*, he writes of a 200-year-old story about Hiero, King of Syracuse, who hired a goldsmith to fashion him a crown. Hiero suspects the goldsmith may have replaced some of the gold with silver. He tasks Archimedes with figuring out the truth, and Archimedes accepts the challenge.

As the story goes, Archimedes was taking a bath while trying to solve the riddle when he realized his body displaced the water. His Eureka Moment came when he realized he could measure the crown against a replica of pure gold. A test was devised, and the king's suspicions were found to be correct. Like most stories over time, this tale has historical errors and fallacies. However, it has endured because of its commonality of experience around A-ha! Moments and the thrill of suspense. We all know what happened to the goldsmith...‹gulp›.

When faced with an impossible problem, it is your responsibility to work as hard and as long as necessary to solve it. No one else is going to do the work for you. However, there are many paths that lead to the mountaintop. One is hard work. Another is smart work. Both are valuable. Opening up opportunities for this unconscious, creative *Default Mode* to work its magic is an example of smart work. What follows is a protocol for intentionally engaging the power of your *Default Mode* in your everyday life.

It is important to note that while going about the hard work of solving your impossible problems, you should also create intentional space for play and relaxation (e.g., putting together a puzzle, walking in the park, doing something with your hands like woodworking or sewing) so your mind has time to rest. In these *Default Modes*, you will give your creative unconscious a chance to solve the problem in unusual ways.

There is another type of work you can do that I call *Deep Listening*. It is a time-limited exercise to unlock your *Default Mode Network* to let it do its thing. It is mind wandering of the highest caliber. Other descriptions of this practice might be the subtle art of intentional daydreaming or intentional, intense relaxation. It exists somewhere between meditation and contemplation.

Anyone who has ever practiced meditation even once knows that if you want to come up with a killer to-do list, all that is needed is to attempt meditation. Every thought you have ever had about anything will suddenly become the most important idea in the world. This is why so many find meditation difficult. Once we pause and pay attention to our monkey minds, we realize our everyday thought life is like a toddler banging a pan with a wooden spoon.

Deep Listening is a strategy for thinking about what you think you already know (e.g., the things you need to do today) and holding a space that allows for deeper more original thoughts to spring forth from your unconscious.

Most people do not fully grasp the magnitude of the power of their unconscious. Our unconscious is perpetually attempting to burst into conscious awareness. It is handicapped because it speaks a different language. Instead of words and logical thoughts, it uses symbols and emotion. The language of the unconscious is most evident in things like our dreams, panic attacks or sudden experiences of intense emotion that surface without any logical source (e.g., crying at a TV commercial).

Deep Listening is an attempt to work our way through the conscious layers of thought down to the more expansive and interconnected layers where original ideas and novel solutions are more likely to occur. Author and critic William Deresiewicz writes:

> It's only by concentrating, sticking to the question, being patient, letting all the parts of my mind come into play, that I arrive at an original idea. By giving my brain a chance to make associations, draw connections, take me by surprise. And often even that idea doesn't turn out to be very good. I need time to think about it, too, to make mistakes and recognize them, to make false starts and correct them, to outlast my impulses, to defeat my desire to declare the job done and move on to the next thing.

Here are the steps for practicing *Deep Listening*:

- Find a quiet place where you will not be disturbed. Bring something to write with and take notes on. At the top of the page write your "prompt." A prompt is a cue to your unconscious regarding what to focus on. It can be general like "Listening" or more specific like "Relationship."

- Set the alarm on your phone for seven minutes. Put a fun, playful chime on your alarm to ease you back into the present. A clanging alarm will disrupt the flow if you want to add additional time.

- Don't focus on your breath. Try to keep your mind as free and open as possible. This is NOT meditation.

- Choose whether you want to practice with your eyes open (trance state) or eyes closed (dark state) listening. If you choose eyes-open listening, stare off into the distance not focusing on any one thing. If you choose eyes-closed listening, simply breathe and relax your body. Mix it up. Experiment. Try eyes open for 3.5 minutes and closed for the last 3.5 and see what works best for you.

- Once you have chosen how to listen, hit the start button on your timer and wait for your first thoughts to appear.

- Write down pertinent thoughts. It isn't necessary to write down *every* thought. Postponing this step will often result in the idea vanishing as quickly as it came.

- What you will discover is that the first layer of thoughts are noise. They consist of the busyness of life like picking up your dry cleaning or signing up to volunteer at your kid's school.

- The second layer is where the unconscious will see its opportunity and start sending the deeper thoughts about your impossible problems. It will cherish the attention you are offering and in return give you a treasure trove of creative ideas.

- Remember, holding a nonjudgmental space is essential to finding flow. Whatever comes up is what comes up.

- If at the end of the seven minutes you feel the need for more time, set another seven minute alarm. When your time feels complete, return to the previous day's list and add anything you didn't get accomplished.

I want to encourage you to take the *30-Day Deep Listening Challenge*. Commit to practicing this exercise five to seven days a week for a month before making a judgment on its effectiveness.

PART 3
TOOLS

21

RELATIONSHIPS – PART I

The Togetherness Matrix

Over the course of my career, there have been moments when years of trial and error converged with knowledge to help clarify a psychological concept that had eluded my understanding. Some of these Eureka Moments have taken the form of illustrations where a picture is truly worth a thousand words.

If there is one area where impossible problems crop up like fireflies at sunset on a hot August day it is the arena of love and relationships. Our romantic relationships are the threshing floor upon which we work out the wounds of childhood, our unbridled teen years and the ignorant bliss of our naïve twenties with the one person we supposedly love more than any other human on earth.

In February 2017 Krista Tippett interviewed Alain de Botton.[1] He had this to say about the impossible problems of romantic relationships:

> When you ask someone to marry you, for example, you're asking someone to be your chauffeur, co-host, sexual partner, co-parent, fellow accountant, mop the kitchen floor together, etc., etc. And on and on the list goes. No wonder that we fail at some of the tasks and get irate with one another. It's a burden. And I think sometimes, the older I get, sometimes I think one of the nicest things you can do to someone you really admire is leave them alone. Just let them go. Let them be. Don't impose yourself on them because you're challenging.

If only letting someone go were so easy.

We cling to anyone who makes us happy and tolerates our shortcomings and eccentricities like a drowning person grasping for a life preserver. When these loved ones threaten to leave us, this puts our happiness in jeopardy, and we become aggressive. We challenge them in ways that are borderline criminal then promise to never do it again. Yet the behaviors repeat themselves with vulgar regularity.

There are many excellent resources available on how to make relationships work. Google "The Gottman Institute"

---

[1] https://onbeing.org/programs/alain-de-botton-the-true-hard-work-of-love-and-relationships-feb2017/

and read everything they have written. I could not compete with the Gottmans and many others like them. I only want to offer a simple tool that can bring clarity to how aligned (or not) you and your partner are in certain areas and which areas may need some attention.

The graphs below represent four important areas of committed, long-term relationships: PROFESSIONAL/PLAY/ROMANTIC/THE GRIND. There are other important areas to be sure, but these are four primary domains.

YOUR TOGETHERNESS MATRIX

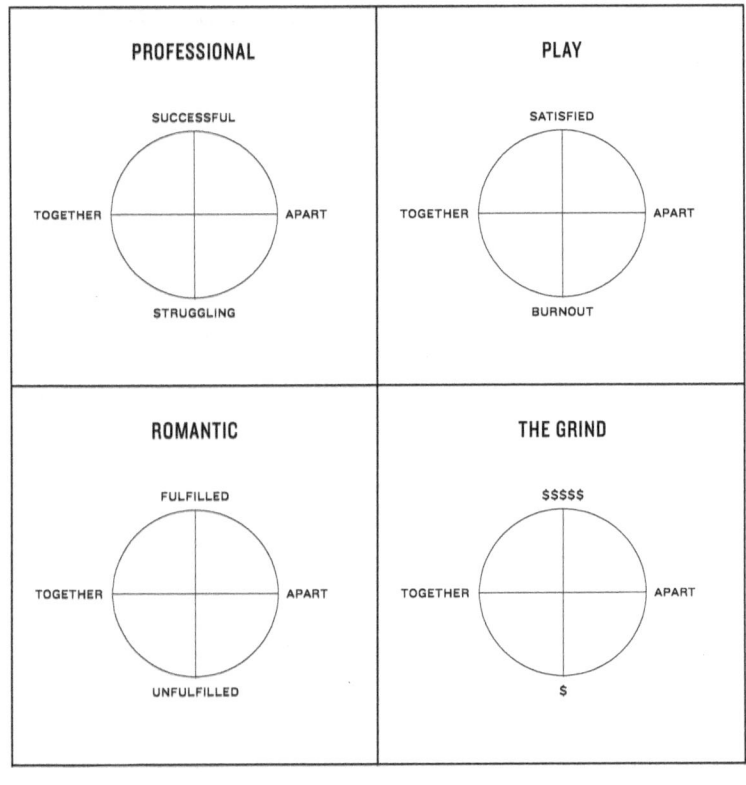

RELATIONSHIPS PART I – THE TOGETHERNESS MATRIX

YOUR PARTNER'S TOGETHERNESS MATRIX

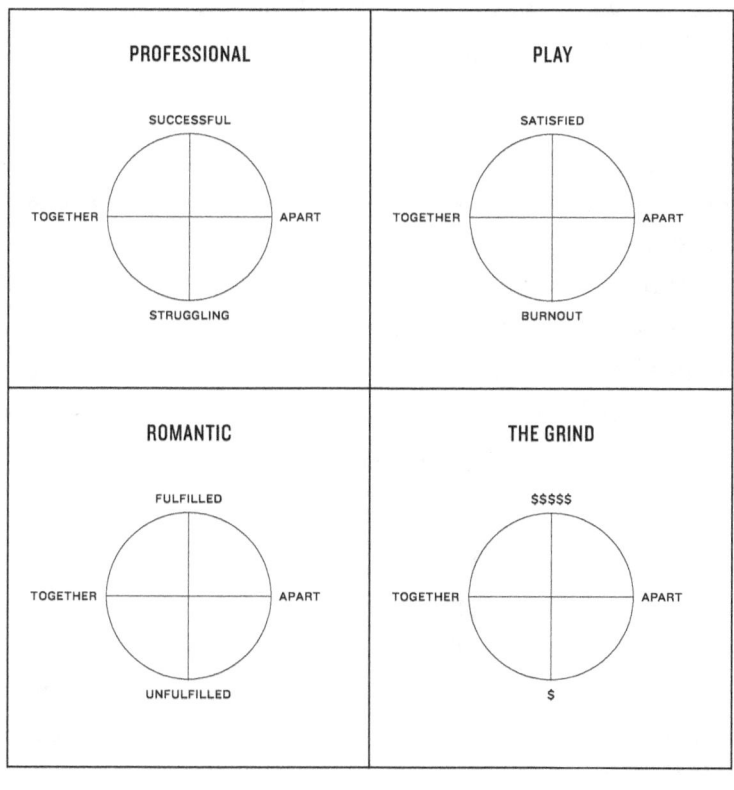

Each partner uses one *Togetherness Matrix* to mark themselves and their partner. The instructions are as follows:

> Place an "X" where you feel you, personally, are in each domain presently. Then grade your partner by placing an "O" in each quadrant that best represents your assessment of where your believe them to be. Once both of you have completed your matrix independently, compare the two to see how aligned you are to one another.

Before you begin, let's take a deeper dive into each of the vertical and horizontal axes. Within each quadrant is a circle bisected by two lines. The horizontal line in each quadrant stays the same. It represents being "TOGETHER" or "APART." Being TOGETHER means the couple is aligned on purpose and values for that category. The couple engages in healthy communication, and when disagreements arise they work them out effectively. When a couple is TOGETHER they are supportive of one another.

In each quadrant, the APART descriptor represents the opposite of being together. The couple is rarely aligned on purpose and/or values. The couple is disconnected in this area and lacks healthy communication. Due to the stress of this dysfunctional dynamic, the couple finds it difficult to support one another.

The vertical axis in each quadrant fluctuates based on the category. For example in the *Professional* category, one person may have a *Successful* career while the other person is *Struggling*. This does not necessarily mean the couple themselves are struggling in this area. The couple can be

TOGETHER even when one person may not be successful in their career.

Context is critical to consider when it comes to each category. One example of a healthy context may be that the unsuccessful person in the relationship is in an untenable work situation that has nothing to do with their romantic relationship. However, a wide gap in the professional lives of two people for a long period of time can be the cause of significant stress and disconnection.

In the *Play* category the vertical axis is represented by "$" to "$$$$$." This category is defined by how much money the couple spends on shared experiences. This is a unique category for each couple. This dynamic is typically worked out while dating. Couples who have widely varying interests rarely stay together for too long. There is simply too little overlap of activities they enjoy.

This issue can become more pronounced the longer a couple stays together. Couples married for decades can grow apart as they differentiate from one another. The threat arises when the couple doesn't make intentional efforts to grow together. A different variation of this threat is when one person tries to include the other, but they are uninterested or apathetic toward what excites their partner. Conversely, couples who play well together over long swaths of time create resilience in their relationship by letting off steam, reconnecting and unplugging from stress.

Clients with little financial means often resist the idea that they need to spend a lot of money to have fun. This is not true, and this is not what the scale intends to represent. The $$$$$ designation is specific to each couple's individual financial situation. For one couple, $$$$$ might represent $100 a month. For a wealthier couple, $$$$$ might represent $10,000 a month. Money doesn't buy happiness, to be sure, but it can provide opportunities that are conducive to happiness (i.e., regular massages, dinner dates, vacations, psychotherapy, couple's retreats, childcare, etc.). If both partners mark APART and spend a small amount of money (relative to their income) on *Play*, that is indicative of deeper issues plaguing the relationship. Couples who cannot figure out how to play together either split up or slowly transition to roommate status.

Closely related to *Play* is *Romantic*. If *Play* is about having fun and relaxing, *Romantic* is about connecting on a deeper level through physical and emotional intimacy. Popular media sensationalizes and sentimentalizes love through music and movies. The "Happily Ever After" stories are "happily" demonized in thoughtful circles as overblown sentimentality, or worse, harmful to our psyche. Yet these stories perennially pop up like dandelions because we are broken people continually looking to other broken people for love and acceptance.

Although this graph does not include the category of spirituality, *Romantic* is close. When many couples are asked how they met, they often say things like, "I knew the moment I saw her she was the one" or "It felt like we had known each other for years, not hours." All these emotions point to something we feel for this particular person.

What could be more spiritual than finding your soul mate or feeling the deepest love you have ever known.

In the *Romantic* quadrant, the *Fulfilled* designation means that your partner pays attention to you, is curious about what goes on in your life on a regular basis and displays a strong desire to be with you physically, emotionally and intellectually.

Paradoxically, when one or both people in the relationship are *Unfulfilled*, sex is typically one of the first casualties followed by a lack of curiosity, disconnection and finally apathy. Like *Play*, if *Romance* is neglected the couple will eventually fall into roommate status.

The Grind. No one can truly understand what *The Grind* means until they have children. We were once free beings with true autonomy and nary a care in the world. Then children enter the scene, and our life ceased to be our own. Most of our energy is redirected toward making sure our children A) don't die and B) learn life skills for their eventual departure. There are a few bouncy house parties, high school sporting events and vacations in between, but most of life as a parent revolves around points A) and B). Interspersed in the fun times are scary ER visits and sleepless nights awake with a sick child. One of the oxymoronic paradoxes of *The Grind* is summarized by Gretchen Rubin's thoughtful, "the days are long but the years are short."

The daily grind will rip a person to shreds. If you don't sleep well, are not exercising, are overstressed at work, rarely see your spouse when you're not drop-dead tired, have sex maybe once a month but have fights once a day, have too much month at the end of the money and vacations are just those things you do where you pack all your stuff but do the same draining routines you do at home in an unfamiliar place without the convenience of knowing where any of your essential items are located...THEN you have come face to face with the abyss known as *The Grind*. If a couple can't do *The Grind* well, they are doomed. It is a snowpack on the precipice of an avalanche that must be constantly monitored for safety, or it will crush the couple without mercy.

For a couple to do *The Grind* well, they must be TOGETHER on issues like who is picking up the kids, who pays what bills, how much money is in the account at any given moment, did we sign the life insurance papers, knowing where the passports are hours before leaving the country, etc. etc. When a couple is APART, life falls apart faster than an overstuffed taco. Even when couples are together, burnout can sweep in like a swarm of locusts with devastating effect.

The threat of *The Grind* comes in two forms: internal and external. One example of an internal threat is when one partner has an affair. External threats are things like an unforeseen job loss or one partner getting a cancer diagnosis.

When both partners are *Satisfied* in this domain, they are a force to be reckoned with. They handle external threats like SEAL Team 6 handled Osama bin Laden. They look out for each other and anticipate the other person's needs. They do their job and do it well. Their credo is: We are on the #SAMETEAM. Nothing outside of us will bring us down.

Satisfied couples face internal threats with compassion and courage...most of the time. They have their "broken wing" moments when they are overwhelmed and need patience and compassion from their partner, but these moments are the exception, not the rule.

As has been repeated many times, every answer to every impossible problem you will ever have must begin with awareness that there is a problem. If after scoring the *Togetherness Matrix* you find that both of you are mostly aligned, then good work! Don't take it for granted. Keep working to stay aligned. Like a garden, relationships need constant care. Time and familiarity have a way of eroding even the best of them. Remember, no matter how *Together* you feel you are in each quadrant, there is always room for improvement.

2 2

RELATIONSHIPS – PART 2

I have a theory about how we form romantic relationships. It begins, as expected, something like this. We meet someone, and we either find them physically attractive or not. If no attraction exists, it never gets off the ground. Once an initial physical attraction is established, an unconscious dance begins.

The unconscious dance deepens through intimate conversations about family, past relationships, movies, music, your best friends, traumatic experiences, career aspirations, where you want to travel, etc. The answers to these questions lead down one of two paths. The first path leads to the couple drifting away from each other. The second path leads to the couple growing closer and deeper. All good so far.

One powerful dynamic of the unconscious dance centers around how each person has been wounded in past relationships, romantic or otherwise. We all get wounded in many different ways by many different people. Some of those wounds were committed maliciously by those who intended us harm. Other wounds are accidental or no one's fault really. It's just life and life isn't fair. But wounds are wounds, and they leave a mark on our psyche that we don't soon forget. These wounds taint our views of others and how much/little we trust and how quickly we choose to trust this person we are now physically attracted to.

As the unconscious dance deepens, and this is where my theory starts to take shape, what happens is that the couple discovers through subtle verbal and nonverbal communication how their wounds are either complimentary or conflicting. Two people who have been wounded in similar ways may find each other attractive and may enjoy each other's company but should never be in a romantic relationship with each other. They sometimes do, and it is often a tragic combination.

To have wounds that are complementary means that the way in which one person has been hurt doesn't conflict with the other person's wounds or beliefs. The other person can hold us and support us in our wounded places because they don't need support in the same way as we do.

One of the greatest gifts we can give another person is to see their wounds without judgment, not be triggered by them and hold a space for that other person to flail on occasion and heal when they are ready. This is what true love feels like.

However, as I have refined my theory, I have witnessed two fatal flaws. The first flaw, if my theory is accurate, is that most relationships are built on the unstable foundation of how one partner's wounds are complemented by the other person's strengths. In other words, we bond over our brokenness.

Initially, this is not a problem. In fact, it feels like the exact opposite. It is in these moments we put on our capes and come to the rescue of our beloved. We blindly believe that our love is so expansive that if our relationship calls us toward heroism, we will make that sacrifice. What higher love could there be than someone seeing our brokenness and loving us in spite of it?

However, this deep sense of being known is actually the undoing of nearly every long-term relationship. As the years grind on, if we don't do the hard work required to heal our wounded parts, the grace our partner extends us becomes tattered and threadbare. Over time this breaks down our partner. They are no longer willing to bear the burden of our unhealed parts if we are not willing to do the work necessary to mature and move past them. In this state, the unhealed parts of our partner that were once the basis for our love become too heavy and threaten to drown us. This is a painful and tragic end that must occur for something better to be built either with our partner or with someone new. The old relationship must die. This, I am convinced, is why the divorce rate hovers around fifty percent. As friend and Episcopal priest Dixon Kinser once noted, "The new thing you are looking for will not be found in the old thing you are leaving."

The second fatal flaw in my relationship theory is that when we are in our 20s and ask someone to marry us, we are ill-prepared to understand ourselves in any significant way or how to convey this lack of self-awareness to this other person. We can't tell them how our immaturity and selfishness will dramatically and negatively impact their life over the long haul. We have even less idea about how life and love will change us, for better or worse, and who we will become because of these experiences. We have no way of knowing at twenty-five how our personality will evolve and what we will value at forty-five.

The promises we make at the altar before friends, family and God are sincere but naïve. They are not shallow. Most of the time we sincerely mean them. But ask anyone who has been married for longer than ten years, and they will tell you they barely recognize, both physically and emotionally, the people in their wedding photos. When we or our partner changes, as all of us are destined to do, it is destabilizing and threatening. Our partner's transformation signals to us that we are not the end all, be all to our partner.

Many young couples falsely and naïvely believe when they say I do they are also saying, "I will be your everything and you will be my everything." That may feel true in the beginning, but as we mature, the thin ice of this belief cracks underneath the weight of reality. Life transforms us in good and bad ways that change our values and desires.

Children transform us in good and bad ways that deepen our ability to love. Our lover transforms us in good and bad ways that we must adapt to or the relationship will surely die a bitter death.

If love is so doomed, as my nihilistic viewpoint suggests, then why even try? What can be done? Truth be told, there is nothing you or anyone else can do about the struggles that age and maturity bring. If you get married in your 20s, your relationship is destined to have several major evolutions.

When your partner changes, it happens on the inside first, out of view of anyone but themselves, and sometimes they don't even recognize it is happening. If you have a trusting relationship and open communication, you may be privy to some of these changes. However, many don't have this type of healthy relationship, and the changes that occur are not communicated in real time. When major shifts occur on the inside of one person while the other person thinks everything is the same based on outward actions, friction and instability happen fast. This instability creates fear and confusion. Isolation creeps into the relationship, which only exacerbates the problem.

Like all impossible problems, the 8 C's are a path forward. Husband and wife team John and Julie Gottman have made some pretty bold predictions on the success and failure of marriages based on their decades, long research on what makes marriages work and what doesn't.

After studying couples closely (and by closely, I mean recording hours of interactions and examining frame by frame—there are 32 frames per second—the couple's facial expressions, dialogues and biometric readings), they discovered a few things about the impossible problems in relationships.

John makes the bold prediction that after watching a couple communicate on pretty much any topic for fifteen minutes, he can guess the possibility of divorce with eighty to ninety percent accuracy. How does he do this? Because he looks for one telltale sign: contempt. Contempt is unconsciously expressed physically with a curling upward of only one side of the top lip. If Mr. Gottman sees this one telltale sign, he knows beyond a shadow of a doubt the couple is in serious trouble.

But that isn't the only discovery he made through his research. The Gottmans uncovered four troubling areas he calls the "four horsemen of the apocalypse."[1] The Biblical reference to the Book of Revelations is intentional as each horseman symbolizes events that herald the end of times. The four horsemen are criticism, defensiveness, stonewalling and contempt.

Criticism refers to making extreme and often absolute statements about the other person, such as "You always" or "You never." Defensiveness refers to deflecting blame that rightfully belongs to you onto your partner or changing the subject to a transgression your partner committed in the past. Stonewalling refers to putting up an invisible barrier between you and your partner in an attempt to protect yourself and/or punish the other person. It is

---

[1] https://www.gottman.com/blog/the-four-horsemen-recognizing-criticism-contempt-defensiveness-and-stonewalling/

characterized in actions by withdrawing, shutting down and/or physically distancing yourself from your partner during intense interactions. Finally, contempt is when you treat your partner with disrespect, disgust or condescension. It is easy to see how a part that is deeply wounded or fearful would respond with any or all of these to someone they feel is threatening them. Do you see your own parts engaging in these four behaviors in your relationship? If so, make a mad dash to your list of 8 C's and begin implementing them in your conversations, your own thoughts and your actions.

One impossible problem I witness on a regular basis is when someone unconsciously chooses the same type of partner over and over. We all have that "friend" that complains of picking the same type of person who then ends up having the same type of problems.

My client Haley complained of repeatedly choosing men who were excessively laid back. The type of man she was attracted to was so laid back that they often didn't have enough money to pay for anything beyond their first date. She convinced herself that she was so "Type A" and high-strung that she needed someone opposite from herself so they could help her relax and have more fun.

When she came to see me, she was on her fourth major relationship, each lasting years. She had just as many car loans to prove it. The painful trap she repeated, much to the chagrin of her friends and family, was her irrational belief that she could rescue these men, like abandoned puppies on the side of the road, and help them get on their feet. None of them had any significant work history, and each one made excuses as to why. If they just had a car, they could go to interviews, get to work, drive for Uber, etc. However, the reality was that while she was working all day, they would go over to their friend's house, play video games and smoke pot.

On one occasion, her boyfriend took the car that she was paying for and used the gas money she gave him to visit a female friend. The two of them ended up having sex. His deception was uncovered when at her annual medical checkup she was diagnosed with a sexually transmitted infection. This is the event that caused her to reach out to me.

Three of the men stopped paying on their loans but kept the cars after the breakup. Being a stickler about her finances, she dutifully paid the loans to avoid ruining her credit. She managed to pay off all the loans with her savings but was bitter about the price she had to pay, literally, to learn her lesson.

Haley was intellectually savvy and explained in detail how she noticed when the patterns in her boyfriends started to emerge. She also acknowledged that she was too emotionally immature to stop the pattern on her own, much like an alcoholic trying to stop drinking by themselves.

She described to me her pattern. After buying her boyfriend a car, she became hypercritical of his laziness. She withheld sex to motivate him, which only worked temporarily. It did not change who he was on a fundamental level. Eventually he blamed her for being manipulative and controlling.

RELATIONSHIPS PART 2

After reading one of the Gottmans books, she was able to identify that, in the end, each boyfriend treated her with criticism, defensiveness, stonewalling and ultimately contempt. She was tired of being blamed for sticking her neck out for someone and receiving little to no appreciation.

After six months of analyzing her personality and attachment style and investigating her self-sacrificing, manipulative parts, Haley was able to identify the false belief that she needed someone laid back. Rather, what she needed was someone who was as strong-willed as herself and driven for success.

Once Haley was able to recognize her unconscious motivations, she sought to intentionally challenge and change her behaviors. This coincided with advances in her career. While on a business trip, she met a CEO named Brian who swept her off her feet.

They dated, fell in love and were engaged within a year of meeting each other. When Brian asked her to marry him, he took her to a Porsche dealership just to "look around." He knew her dream car was a Porsche Panamera. When they took it for a test drive, Brian planned ahead and had her engagement ring attached to the key ring with a note that said, "This is yours. Will you be mine?"

Let's pause for a moment in Haley's story. Did any part of you get triggered by her "Happily Ever After" ending? Did you feel a sense of excitement for Haley because things worked out so well after doing so much of the hard work of happiness? Did you feel jealous of her good fortune? Or both? Did a skeptical part of you leap up and protest, "This doesn't happen in real life! You made this story up?" It is true that these events didn't happen in exactly this way. I have to protect the privacy of clients, so I changed the details. Does it calm your parts down knowing this was "make believe"? What if in reality it was a house she was given or a vacation? Or a boat? Or a million-dollar race horse? Would that make any difference to your parts?

I haven't seen Haley in years, but I suspect her relationship didn't turn out to be all unicorns and rainbows. What if Brian's job that allowed him to pay cash for a $100,000 car also kept him away from home three weeks out of the month? Wouldn't that get old fast?

Impossible problems in relationships are impossible to avoid. How well you understand the various parts of you that get triggered and why can make all the difference.

23

ANXIETY – PART I

The Non-Stop Brain

Sophia sat on my couch, nibbling on what remained of her eviscerated fingernails. At twenty-four she had passed the age by which she thought she would have reached several significant milestones. She wasn't going outside during the day, and her pale face was evidence of her isolation.

A year ago, she broke up with a man she thought she was going to marry. Since then dating had been a disaster. Every guy she met on one of her many dating apps wanted one thing, and it wasn't a lasting, meaningful relationship. She went on several dates with friends of friends, but they were all bland as tapioca pudding. More than one of them confessed their undying love for her after the end of their first date.

She didn't finish college because she was in a punk rock band that signed a record deal at the end of her junior year. The band toured that summer, which was a huge success. They were set to embark on several festival gigs until the lead singer was placed in rehab after an episode of a possible suicide attempt by illicit drug overdose.

Sophia's parents could not afford to pay for her final year of college. If she wanted to return, she would have to take out student loans. While she liked her classes, she did not want to pay the hefty $50,000 for a liberal arts degree. She toyed with the idea of touring as a solo artist but didn't have the money to fund a band, and playing on stage alone with a guitar scared her senseless.

Sophia's latest boyfriend was hot and cold. On occasion he would make her feel beautiful and smart. This calmed her down and made her feel like she could tackle all her problems and come out a winner. Then he would vanish for days with no calls and no texts, only to reappear as if nothing had happened.

She hated being so emotionally dependent on him. The truth was that she literally had no one else in her life who seemed to care about her outside of her brother and her parents.

Just before the session, Sophia texted her boyfriend who, as predicted, did not reply. She kept her phone on her knee obsessively checking it.

"Ugh! Why am I like this? This isn't me. I don't act like an immature teenager when a boy doesn't return my text. Yet here I am acting like a pathetic teenager when my boyfriend doesn't return my text."

We sat in silence for a few moments.

"I mean seriously. I don't sleep. I'm depressed. My bandmates don't return my calls either. It's like we're all pissed at each other about Missy's...whatever she did. No matter what I do my brain doesn't stop. It just won't let me relax. Can you fix me?" she says half laughing, half serious.

Over the past few years, I have had a growing compassion for clients who suffer from anxiety and anxiety disorders. There are two forms of anxiety: situational and organic. Examples of an anxiety-producing situation might be a child witnessing their parents argue in a domestic violence situation. A more biologically driven anxious situation might involve a person's irrational fear of entering a building with a revolving door. They cannot overcome the dreadful thoughts of getting trapped in the enclosed space with the germs on the glass and push bar if the door were to stop or get jammed. As a result this person must use the stairs in the rear of the building each day to get to work.

In either case, the resulting symptoms are overwhelming bodily sensations that cause extreme discomfort. It is no wonder so many people turn to alcohol and drugs, both prescription and illicit, to suppress the symptoms even though they know it is not the most healthy solutions... but they work.

The domain I am most familiar with in regard to anxiety is the mind. The symptom I hear about more than any other is what my clients call their *Non-Stop Brain*.

Like Sophia, anxious individuals engage in a litany of tiresome activities like reviewing conversations they had throughout the day to make sure they didn't say anything offensive. Even after their review turns up no potential transgressions, they continue to whip themselves into a frenzy. They convince themselves they need to text the person to confirm that everything is okay. If their friend/family member/ romantic partner/coworker doesn't respond in a timely manner, their anxiety fills in the blank space with a host of terrible possibilities. If this crazy-making isn't stopped when it first tries to take root, it will spiral out of control quickly, ruining an otherwise pleasant and peaceful day.

The term for creating terrible scenarios based on little to no factual information is called *catastrophizing*. This distressing behavior creates imaginary scenarios that increase anxiety, then trick the mind into believing they are true. This vicious cycle causes untold amounts of unnecessary suffering.

What I have identified in a large number of clients is what I would call a *Roaming Anxiety* part. My experience with men, women, young and old is that those who suffer from anxiety on a daily basis have a part that restlessly scans the internal and external environment searching for something, anything, to be anxious about. It might be an inattentive boyfriend or girlfriend who regularly ignores texts. It might be a terrible event on the news that the person keeps watching for hours on end. It might be the rumors at work that there will be big layoffs right before the holidays.

Ironically, what I have also identified is that when this *Roaming Anxiety* part finds nothing to latch onto, which is rare, it becomes agitated. It is as if the part *knows* there is something wrong, but it isn't looking hard enough. Since there is nothing to be anxious about *right now*, then it must be anxious about not being anxious.

Here is an example of a frequent conversation an anxious person will have with themselves:

Anxious Part: "Something's wrong."

Person: "What?"

Anxious Part: "Something."

Person: "What!"

Anxious Part: "Some! Thing!"

Because the sensation of anxiety presents so strongly in the body, it often overwhelms other more subtle parts that need attention but don't create as much fuss. When someone feels they are about to have a panic attack at a business lunch, they aren't concerned about analyzing the irrationality of their fear and where it originated. The number one task is to get rid of the distressing sensations and return to normal without embarrassing themselves and losing a potential new client.

What, then, is there to do with this *Roaming Anxiety* part? The simplest explanation is to fight back. When the spark of worry starts smoldering, it will burn your house down in a very short period of time if you do not extinguish the emotional flames while they are manageable. One strategy is to assess an anxiety-producing situation based on four criteria: important, unimportant, urgent, not urgent.

If you will allow your Logical part to help you during anxious moments, which it so desperately wants to do, with practice you can begin restructuring your habit of worry to quickly assess if the situation warrants either "Action" or "Asking For Help" or "Let It Go." This will not be an easy habit to change at first, but it will give you something else to do besides spinning in circles worrying yourself to death (this is not a metaphor).

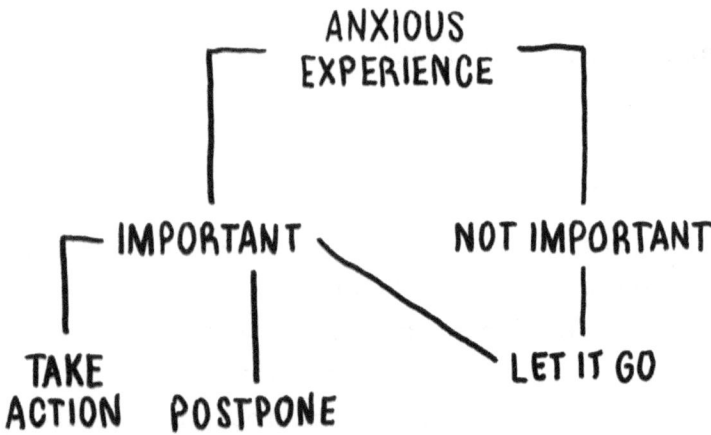

What might this *Anxiety Flow Chart* look like in action?

Take Michelle, for example. She is a Type 6 on the Enneagram with a high Self-Preservation instinct. The Type 6s come prewired with an anxious stance toward life. She is Introverted and has an Anxious Attachment. She has one-and-a-half-year-old twin boys. She had a career for years as a voiceover artist for commercials as well as an audiobook reader. She decided to put her career on pause until her boys were in school.

Michelle loves being with her boys but did not anticipate how much time she would have alone. Her husband, Leo, leaves at 6:00 A.M. and works until 6:00 P.M. each night. They both realize this arrangement doesn't fit their lifestyle, but no easy changes can be made currently.

Michelle had a difficult day with the boys. They wouldn't nap and wouldn't eat and were loud and fussy all day, wearing her down emotionally. Michelle is typically patient with her boys, but today she didn't have it in her to give.

At 6:15 P.M. when Leo had still not arrived home, she felt that familiar anxious energy starting to build. She texted him to find out where he might be. His response was terse, "I'll be late." This did nothing to assuage Michelle's anxiety and only increased her anger.

When Leo finally arrived home at 7:30 P.M. talking on his phone, she became irate. She refused to make eye contact with him and left him to take a hot bath, mumbling to herself that he could make his own dinner. Twenty minutes later, her husband entered the bathroom after putting the boys, to bed knowing he is about to get an earful. He walks in and leans against the vanity.

"Why are you angry with me?" Michelle barks at him.

"Let me guess. My text made you angry, and now you are going to punish me for being late for not giving you a three-page explanation. You know, sometimes I just wish you could act like a grownup and stop thinking that every time something doesn't work out perfectly that I'm cheating on you or I'm dead."

Michelle slinks down in the bath water until her face is covered up to her nose. A tear slides down her face.

Her husband softens, "Here's what happened. When I left work, the car started making that terrible sound again. The one where the mechanic told me if it happened again to immediately bring it back because it could cause major damage. So I drove directly to the mechanic shop. On my way there, I got an emergency call from the Manhattan client who never received the documents I Fedex'd yesterday for the premiere tonight. In the middle of that conversation, my phone ran out of battery. When I was finally able to charge it in the parking lot of the mechanic, I saw your text and immediately responded, got an Uber and called my client back. The Uber driver didn't have an extra cord for my phone, so I had to risk running out of battery again while talking to my client. That's what I was doing on my way home."

"I'm sorry," Michelle managed.

"I know you are, but I need someone who will trust me and support me not punish me. This is too exhausting."

Here is a list of issues happening in this moment for this couple:

- *The Grind* is wearing this couple thin.
- Michelle is *Unsatisfied* with her choice to leave her career.

She is feeling isolated and slightly depressed.

- Michelle is having a *Broken Wing* moment and needs her husband to take care of her.

- Michelle's *Type 6 Personality and Anxious Attachment* are causing her to catastrophize, which only exacerbates the problem.

- Leo is a Type 5 on the Enneagram and has difficulty dealing with overblown emotional responses to logical situations. He is *Securely Attached* with a high *Self-Preservation Instinct*.

The list goes on and on about how this scenario is the perfect storm for a marital spat. However, what might this scenario have looked like if the moment Michelle didn't get the response she wanted that instead of going to anger and anxiety she forced herself to walk through the steps of the *Anxiety Flow Chart*?

She took immediate action when she was concerned and reached out to Leo. He responded as soon as he could that he would be late. If Michelle could have registered that A) Leo responded and is safe, B) he would be late and calmed herself down in that moment, C) greeted him when he arrived with patience or humor (e.g., holding up a sign when he walked in the door that read "Your wife is trapped inside this zombie. She needs help!") Had she willed herself to overcome her anxiety, fear and frustration, the rest of the night might have turned out differently with each person being more able and willing to care for the other person. In reality they were both having difficult days.

Michelle spent an hour cooking dinner before Leo arrived. How loving would it have been to Leo and herself if she could have acknowledged but not surrendered to her anxious, angry parts and instead enjoyed a peaceful, relaxing dinner later when his work was completed? It would have been an epic feat for her to calm herself in the moment. Yet that is exactly what the hard work of happiness looks like in real life.

Anxiously Attached individuals are hypersensitive to a person's tone of voice or any variation in the normal routine. Unlike most people, anxious individuals notice each small nuanced piece of information, then take them to the nth degree of worst-case scenarios. This is exhausting to the anxious person and eventually wears the *Exhausted Partner* down to a frazzled nub.

If the *Exhausted Partner* cannot or does not want to tolerate this unrelenting behavior, they will leave the relationship if possible. If leaving is not an option (e.g., the anxious person is your sister) or they do not want to leave (e.g., the anxious person is your husband), then the *Exhausted Partner* will do everything they can to avoid behaviors or conversations that trigger the anxious person. This avoidance strategy works for new romantic relationships but only for a period of time. The longer the anxious behavior continues, the less tolerant the *Exhausted Partner* becomes.

One ironic cycle I witness is when an *Anxiously Attached* individual overwhelms their partner again and again with a tidal wave of emotion and accusations. It is as if the *Anxiously Attached* individual is trying to transfer their angst to their partner. The *Exhausted Partner* absorbs the emotional impact from their partner, which throws them into an emotional crisis of their own. Out of sheer desperation or protest, the *Exhausted Partner* then commits some legitimate offense in an effort to take care of themselves or subconsciously sabotage the relationship. These offenses might include having an emotional or sexual affair or becoming secretive about benign plans to avoid the inevitable arguments if they try to create healthy space between themselves and their anxious partner. These types of responses cause unnecessary suffering in the relationship. If the *Exhausted Partner* could find the courage to confront the unhealthy cycle, they might be able to work through the issues or avoid them altogether.

However, often the problems seem so overwhelming the *Exhausted Partner* doesn't know what to do. If the anxious person finds out about these indiscretions, it validates every fear they have ever had. They extrapolate these isolated indiscretions over their entire relationship, creating an environment of fear. The truth is that the anxious behavior played a significant role in pushing their partner away and contributing to the breakdown. These types of scenarios are complicated and often result in the *Exhausted Partner* fostering a growing contempt for the *Anxiously Attached* individual.

—

I witness a tremendous amount of unnecessary suffering when people try to change some aspect of themselves they don't like that is unchangeable. Michelle could not banish her anxiety by sheer will. She tried and failed many times.

We all have things that we don't like about ourselves. Maybe it's the shape of our noses or our laugh or some darker perversion that causes us shame and embarrassment. We diligently try to scrub them from our humanity but to no avail.

If, like Michelle's anxiety, we cannot fundamentally change some aspect of ourselves after years or maybe decades of trying, then what can be done? Accept who you are right now today, what your specific needs are in a relationship and work to root out unhealthy and disruptive thought patterns and habitual behaviors.

Eleanor Longden talks about realizing she was schizophrenic after a frightening episode of hearing voices one day while in college. Her eventual diagnosis led to a ten-year battle between herself and the medical system that resulted in her losing her autonomy and sense of self. She became suicidal at one point. She was eventually united with a group of caring health professionals who literally saved her life. She could not do anything about the fact that she was schizophrenic, but she could adapt her life to meet this challenge with a new resolve and resources. She honors those who helped her along her journey in her TED Talk[1]:

> [T]ogether, they forged a blend of courage, creativity, integrity, and an unshakeable belief that my shattered self could become healed and whole. I used to say that these people saved me, but what I now know is they did something even more

[1] https://www.ted.com/talks/eleanor_longden_the_voices_in_my_head

> important in that they empowered me to save myself, and crucially, they helped me to understand something which I'd always suspected: that my voices were a meaningful response to traumatic life events, particularly childhood events, and as such were not my enemies but a source of insight into solvable emotional problems.

At some point in her healing journey, Eleanor accepted that she was and always would be schizophrenic. It was a fact. But how courageous and creative to then see those voices as parts of her that were trying to help her in the only way they knew how. She describes how she still hears the voices. She says that now when they tell her if she leaves her apartment that she will be murdered, she knows that what they are really trying to communicate is that she is nervous about something and that she needs to pause and pay attention. She thanks the voices for their input, then seeks out the actual object of her stress and anxiety.

Once you accept who you are in this present moment (anxious, schizophrenic, unemployed, single, broke, heartsick, disabled, depressed), then you can begin to adapt your life to your reality.

An example of this adaptation might be an alcoholic. Once someone accepts that they are an alcoholic, they must then adapt their life to this new reality or suffer the consequences. One way an alcoholic might adapt their life to the reality of their addiction is to stop living in secret and tell their partner, their best friend and their family. Next would be to attend Alcoholics Anonymous meetings, find a therapist, get a sponsor and work on the 12 Steps.

Another way of adapting themselves to being an alcoholic would be to either remove all the alcohol from the home or, if they live with someone who wants to continue to drink, then put the alcohol in a locked cabinet, drive a different route home from work so they don't pass the bar where they stopped each night, don't hang around friends that frequently drink. All these are strategies of adaptation and an example of the hard work of happiness.

Finally, for those who struggle with a *Non-Stop Brain*, you must create a space in your life to experiment with solutions. There are countless methods you can try to see what works for you and your schedule. Here are ten ways to cope with an anxious mind:

- **Drink Tea**—soothing teas like chamomile and herbal blends in the morning and before bed. Light soothing candles made of lavender at night.

- **Don't Watch TV**—an hour before bed, rather read or write something funny, educational or inspirational.

- **Educate Yourself On Ways To Reduce Anxiety & Stress** (e.g., *Mindfulness-Based Stress Reduction Workbook For Anxiety* by Bob Stahl)

- **Meditate**—on your own or with a group and read *10% Happier* by Dan Harris.

- **Find Creative Ways To Challenge Your Anxiety** (e.g., Michelle's Anxiety Awareness Scale)

- **Find A Psychotherapist**

- **Challenge Catastrophic And/Or Black and White**

Thinking—do NOT give them the freedom to spin out of control. If you do allow them to spin out of control then offer the parts of you compassion once you calm down and respond with a positive "we'll get 'em next time" attitude.

- **Be Grateful**—maybe the number one strategy for combating unimportant, non-urgent negative thoughts. It is not possible to worry and be grateful in the same moment.

- **Face Your Fears**—there is an entire chapter on facing fears, and this strategy offers an extremely high return yet is also one of the most difficult to do. Start by facing small fears and build up to bigger fears over time. After all is said and done, this is what the hard work of happiness will require of you.

- **Get In Touch With Your Body**—the reality is that most people can deal with anxious thoughts. What causes the biggest problem is how the anxiety feels in their body. When you are scared, anxious, nervous you feel that in the form of adrenalin, cortisol and all the other stress hormones rushing through your body. This feels terrible. That's why people drink and take drugs (illicit and prescribed). They want to escape the sensations in their body. There are a plethora of ways to connect with the body, including tai chi, qigong, yoga, therapeutic massage, sensory deprivation float tanks, dancing, acupuncture, cranial sacral body work, Reiki, heart rate variability biofeedback or gyrokinesis.

2 4

ANXIETY – PART 2

The Anxiety Spiral: Catch It Early, Catch It Often

Throughout history anxiety served as a survival instinct. As such it was adaptive by its very nature. As our prefrontal cortex evolved and our societies advanced, the primal need to run away from saber-toothed tigers diminished. What took the place of ferocious man-eating animals were threats such as natural disasters, serial killers and the *always more* stress of a consumer driven society.

However, the more primal remnants of our instinctual anxiety have not had enough time to completely fade from our genes. Moreover, some primal instincts like our fight-or-flight response continue to be valuable up to a point. As with any trait, some people have more anxiety than others. These anxious individuals often are pushed along by an invisible force to do and say things they know are not healthy or logical.

For example, when you apply superficial solutions such as distraction (e.g., watching excessive TV, abusing alcohol) to alleviate anxiety, it might work for the moment, but it is not taking the actual problem seriously. Furthermore, because you don't feel anxious doesn't mean the anxiety and the source of it are eliminated. In fact, the opposite is true, resulting in an even more pernicious problem.

Anxiety adapts to its surroundings. This was necessary for ancient tribes living in open spaces with little defense against the elements and animals. Nowadays, when you refuse to face the saber-tooth tiger type problems of a bad marriage, financial bankruptcy or addiction, they don't vanish. They go deep in your subconscious where they are certain to return in unsuspecting and undesired ways such as sexual dysfunction, hives, melancholy, dysthymia, lack of energy, suicidal and homicidal thoughts, anger, etc.

One incredibly effective strategy for coping with an anxious mind is understanding *The Anxiety Spiral*. All of us engage in *catastrophizing* (fixating on the worst possible outcome) from time to time: when our spouse is not home from work at their regular time or when we are forced to have a daunting conversation with our boss over our lackluster performance. We use *catastrophizing* as a way to prepare ourselves for what realistically could be a difficult experience. If we are prepared for difficulty, we tell ourselves, we can handle it better than if we are unprepared.

On the other hand, people who are biologically predisposed to a higher degree of anxiety than most are more likely to engage in this activity on a routine basis. It is their curse. Their *Roaming Anxiety* can literally find anything to freak out about. Below is *The Anxiety Spiral*.

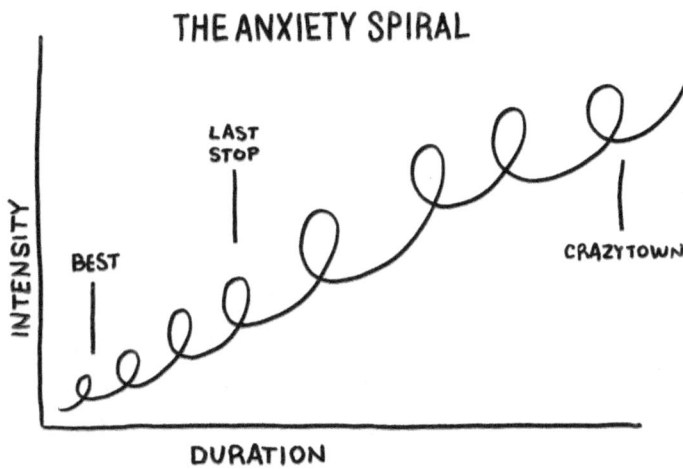

There are two strategies for coping on *The Anxiety Spiral*. The first option is best summarized by Barney Fife, the hapless, good-natured sidekick of Andy Griffith on *The Andy Griffith Show*, who was fond of saying, "Nip it in the bud!" This can be difficult as anxiety is sneaky. It will almost always initially come as a friend whispering important messages about your health and safety. However, this soothing friend quickly transforms into a panic monster. This first option is your best option by far. Another name for this strategy is *Catch It Early. Catch It Often*.

Catch It Early. Catch It Often. requires discipline, willpower and grit. No other mental malady is better suited for *Catch It Early. Catch It Often.* than anxiety. Here is the good—no make that great—news: The more you practice catching your anxious spiral early, the easier it becomes. Like any skill, the more you practice, the more proficient you become. The better you become at detecting your anxiety's wily ways, the more you can adapt yourself to its strategies. The brilliance of *Catch It Early. Catch It Often.* is that it doesn't give your psyche time to maneuver. It shuts down *The Anxiety Spiral* before it has a chance to elude your problem solving strategies.

The other option besides *Catch It Early. Catch It Often.* is to let your anxiety run its course. You have been down this road many times before. You know it won't kill you. It is uncomfortable and you despise it. However, it is also a familiar way of coping with stress. I mean really, you could be chain-smoking instead, right?

Notice the three inflection points on *The Anxiety Spiral* chart. They are Best, Last Stop and Crazytown.

OPPORTUNITY #1: BEST

This is the best-case scenario for catching, stopping and preventing anxiety from spinning out of control. You catch it early here and determine whether or not it is worth your time and energy. If it is worthy, then you tend to the circumstances as best as possible to either solve the problem and/or alleviate the symptoms.

If the offending anxiety is not worth your time, you can kindly dismiss it using any of the ten helpful strategies from the previous chapter. You can also try and peek behind the curtain of anxiety to figure out the root causes of the present angst.

OPPORTUNITY #2: LAST STOP

This is where most people will succeed in terminating their anxious loop. Opportunity #1 is definitely achievable, but it takes a lot of practice, mindfulness and *Self Energy*. Opportunity #2 is when the anxiety has lingered a while and the storm clouds are forming on the horizon. Maybe you are aware of these sensations, or maybe you were too distracted by life to notice. In this stage the body starts to react to the internal stress through tense shoulders, fingernail biting, shallow breathing, sweating, increased heart rate, nausea, etc.

It is not a full-blown anxiety attack yet, but it is heading in that direction. If you catch your anxious thoughts here, it will prevent them from growing from cute little furry beasts into demons with horns, pitchforks and glowing red eyes.

Catching anxious thoughts at this stage is still a challenge that requires attention and practice. It is easy to fall into the trap of believing you can control them. "This time," you convince yourself, "I've got this. I won't let them get out of control." But then comes *Crazytown*.

CRAZYTOWN

Every anxious person I have ever met is intimately acquainted with *Crazytown*. It has ruined so many moments from dates to business opportunities to sleep.

If the anxious person doesn't stop the train somewhere around Opportunity #2, it starts to gain momentum. When anxious thoughts gain momentum, they slip out of our hands like a wet iPhone without a case. What moments ago had been a nice dinner date with your husband turned into an epic fight because you knew he was looking over your shoulder at an attractive woman you saw just before you sat down. But you don't pick a fight about the attractive woman. That would be too easy. When you make it to *Crazytown*, you start talking about how he should be making more money and how he has let himself go and should exercise more. You have no idea he saw a car nearly hit a pedestrian through the restaurant window. His reaction was relief that the person didn't get hit, not his attraction to the female stranger that you assumed.

Crazytown is no fun for anybody. It is a place where good times go to die. But it is a common reality for anxious individuals. The key to coping with an anxious mind is to collect a workshop full of tools to stave off the unnecessary suffering. Then, one-by-one, pull out each tool and practice like a woodworker learning his trade until new habits develop. Your lovers, friends and family will thank you, I promise. And you will be much happier.

25

FACING YOUR FEARS

Her words assaulted me like brass knuckles on bare teeth. I was stunned into silence. After working for a decade in the trenches with suffering individuals, it was no small feat for me to be silenced by a client. Maybe it was the gentle tone of her voice juxtaposed over such a diabolical manifestation of the triumph of evil over good.

I had only recently met this woman with a handful of sessions under our belts prior to this seminal moment. Although I didn't know her well, what I did know is that she was a broken, desperate woman hungry for a better life. In previous sessions, she recounted abusive experiences beginning in her early childhood and continuing up to her most recent boyfriend that ended less than a year before.

On this day in a small community mental health clinic in rural Tennessee crammed into my supply closet turned office, she spoke with a confident yet soft gentility. She was a paradox of tenderness and strength. She was strong enough to have survived her life and courageous enough to recognize at this point she needed help.

In this session, she was listing off her abusers and their transgressions. She started with her mother who abandoned her as a small child. It is hard to imagine how a drug-addicted, prostitute of a mother could have been better for her than the woman who became her guardian, but it was entirely possible. Sometimes neglect is better than attention. This wicked guardian who professed to "love" this little child and dote on her in the presence of others would physically assault her, sexually abuse her and psychologically torture her behind closed doors. This was the context of the conversation when she uttered the worst sentence I have ever heard from any client before or since. She candidly commented as if it were any other casual fact about her life, "It is easier for me to get punched in the face than it is to be loved." Her words tore into me. That one sentence changed her life...and mine.

We went on to work together for the next year. In the pantheon of all the clients I have ever had, it is hard to say which is my favorite but this woman ranks near the top. I can say for certain that I have never had a client before or since work harder to heal her wounds and seek true happiness through loving herself than this woman.

She lived in a small trailer and made do with very little furniture. Sometimes her appliances worked and sometimes they didn't. Sometimes her car worked and sometimes it didn't. But she never once made an excuse and never missed an appointment. She also never missed a day of work. She simply did what had to be done to solve her problem. She worked for years at a chain store that made foot-long sandwiches. She had a daughter who had a seven-year-old son with oppositional defiant disorder whom she was raising because her daughter had neither the emotional nor financial means to care for her child and therefore abandoned him, literally, on her doorstep.

Evidence of this woman's dedication to her healing and growth were everywhere. I have distinct memories during sessions of being humbled by her dedication and tenacity. I often give clients homework in the form of books to read, TED Talks to watch or other random items like articles or research studies. It never occurred to me that someone wouldn't be able to afford a book or have access to the internet. At the very least, they could go to the library, I thought.

It wasn't until this client that I realized some people do not have the luxury of extra money to buy books, much less afford a monthly internet bill. It didn't occur to me that a library in a rural county has far fewer titles and resources than a library in a metropolitan city like Nashville. It didn't occur to me that some people have neither the extra money for gas nor the energy after standing on their feet for ten hours a day at fifty years of age while raising a young child to pick up a book at the library. In spite of all these obstacles, this woman persevered and found a way to complete the homework I assigned her. Here is how this client gamed the system.

This client did not have a fancy iPhone. She had a phone that looked similar to a gray brick. It was large. It was heavy. It had actual buttons. For all of its bulk, it had the tiniest of screens with the lowest possible resolution. Before I knew the circumstances of her life, I gave her homework that seemed relevant to her situation. She shared in session how much she enjoyed the books I assigned. She then began to inform me about highly acclaimed books I had never read. It wasn't until months later that I discovered her secret.

She could not afford to buy books but she wanted to comply with my homework instructions. Rather than purchasing the books, she would find the books I recommended on Amazon and read the free excerpts on her tiny screen. Once she had exhausted the ten or so pages allowed in the free preview, she would scroll down to the recommended section and read the free portion of those books. She kept repeating this process over and over. She was determined, to say the least. This is but one example of her tenacious creativity and perseverance.

Working with this client never felt like "work." It wasn't always easy or fun, but it was always rewarding. I wish I could instill the determination and courage this client carried with her to every one of my clients. It was an honor to work with her.

Pain changes us. It makes no difference if it is physical or emotional. Often our response to pain is to create such vast defense mechanisms as to never again suffer the same indignity. The problem with this all too common strategy is that evil is adaptive by nature. We can never build enough defenses to guard against all the ways in which life will hurt us. Our response to pain reveals the contours of our inner landscape. Do we live in fear seeing potential danger everywhere? Do we see the worst in every person and situation? Do we respond by giving up? Getting angry? Is it possible to see pain as an opportunity to learn about ourselves and/or help others in their time of need? Is it even possible to use terrible, horrible experiences for our benefit?

After more than a decade and a half of working with earnest, good-hearted individuals, I have come to the conclusion that once all the words have been spoken, books read, tears cried and secrets brought into the light, the path to healing comes down to facing our fears. Sometimes these fears are real, and other times these fears are imagined. Both types of fears elicit the same psychological and physiological response in the mind and body.

When we refuse to face our fears, we miss opportunities to reveal our strength and prevail over what has repressed us for so long. Instead we are overcome by fear, anxiety and depression. However, facing our fears is tribulation unto liberation unto happiness. What fears do you need to face today? What people or situations are you avoiding that need to be stared down?

Some people are built for head-to-head battles with their demons. Others are more suited to a different kind of warfare. You can confront your abuser if you want, but it isn't necessary. What if you wrote them a letter and burned it? Or mailed it? Or you filed charges against them? What impossible problems are you ignoring because you are not yet willing to make the sacrifices necessary to achieve the outcome you most desire? Those impossible problems of yours aren't going anywhere. They have been around a long time. The only way you will be rid of them is to put your fears to the side, pick up the 8 C's and face them. When you succeed, and you will surely succeed, you will be free AND you will be happy.

In his inspired letter to those living in Rome around 58 A.D., Saint Paul sent an encouraging reminder across the millennia that continues to be relevant to us today, "Do not let evil get the upper hand, but conquer evil by doing good."

2 6

YOUNG MAN/OLD MAN

Once after a tragic loss, a young man walked into the wilderness leaving behind all he knew and loved. He lived near the top of a mountain above the tree line in a small shelter fashioned from tree limbs and scrub brush. After years on the mountain, he was still young in years but appeared aged with his ruddy, sun-scarred face, long disheveled, dreadlocked hair and matted beard peppered with dust and debris. His clothes were filthy and tattered with crudely patched holes in the knees and elbows. The soles of his boots were strapped to the leather with duct tape from a long since expired roll. His hands were calloused and cracked. His eyes were both vacant and full of pain.

He only ventured from his shelter to scavenge for parts of food undigested by animals. There was neither little shade in the heat of the day nor much warmth on cold nights. The animals and insects were a constant burden.

Years ago when he first arrived on the mountain, the young man constructed a circular labyrinth of stones. Each day upon leaving his shelter he laid a few more rocks, widening the spherical maze. Endlessly he walked round and round his labyrinth until the sun set, signaling it was time for him to return home.

One day while hiking, an elderly man happened upon the young man. He perched himself on a nearby boulder and while eating an apple watched as the young man marched round and round in what appeared to the elderly hiker as mindless wandering. After half an hour, he called out to the young man, "What are you doing?"

"Trying to find my way out of this labyrinth," the young man replied.

"I thought the point of a labyrinth was to get to the center," remarked the old man good-humoredly.

"I have no problem getting to the center," said the young man pointing to his shelter, "It's the getting out that is so difficult. But the mountain gods have a path out. If I keep walking every day they will grant me freedom."

"Mountain gods?" mumbled the old man to himself thinking the young man must be teetering on the edges of sanity. Confused, he finally suggested, "Why don't you just step over the little stone wall? It's only a foot or so high."

The young man flew into a rage, screaming at the old hiker, "Leave me alone, you old, decrepit fool! You should know better than to harass strangers."

The old man packed his food and left as requested.

The young man continued walking his labyrinth grumbling about the old hiker's cruelty, "Just step over the wall. That doesn't make any sense."

As the sun set, the young man's complaining turned to tears. He collapsed on the ground, exhausted. He had not wept in a very long time and could not comprehend why he was so distraught now. He blamed the old hiker though he could not say why.

As the sun was descending into the horizon, the young man stood up to return to his shelter guided by the waning vesper light. In that moment, a wind swept up from the valley, knocking the young man off balance. He turned to steady himself but the crusty film left by the tears distorted his vision. He stepped awkwardly on a stone and twisted his ankle. His foot caught the edge of a jagged rock and sent him hurling to the ground, dashing his head against the pointy edge of the wall, knocking him unconscious.

The young man woke hours later lying on the ground. When he tried to stand, his head pounded in unison with his heart. He slowly lowered himself back to the ground, trying to avoid the sharp daggers of pain shooting through his temples. While trying to stand up, he sensed a storm gathering in the dark distance. Fearful of hypothermia, the young man struggled to stand. Dizzy and in pain he knew he must get to his shelter. The ravenous animals would soon be on the prowl looking to fill their aching bellies. They were typically more scared of him than he of them, but if they smell his blood, who knows what primal instinct might take over. If he could make a small fire before the rain moved in, he could boil water and tend to his wounds. He also knew the smoke and fire might keep the animals at bay.

As he struggled to lift himself, he realized with great horror that he was, in fact, outside of his labyrinth. Fear contorted his chest as he staggered around, searching for his walking staff and satchel of dried berries.

A short distance away, he spied his walking staff and cherished pouch of food. Leaning to pick up his staff, the faint flickering of undulating shadows on a distant rock wall caught his eye. He felt he might be in danger, unsure of what to do. He wondered if he might be hallucinating. Finally convincing himself that he was indeed of sound mind, he became angry. He knew he might have to protect himself from thieves or marauders. Boldly he marched toward the opening in the rock, ready to confront the trespasser. A rolling thunder mixed with the howling of wolves created what looked to him like a comically bad movie set. He paused, frozen by indecision. He desperately wanted to return to his shelter but knew he must get rid of whoever had violated his sacred space.

As he edged closer to the flickering light, he saw a small opening. He entered the opening with his staff ready to attack. As he haltingly entered the cave jabbing his staff ahead of him like a spear, he was surprised to find a small fire lighting the diminutive hideaway with a soft auburn glow. Situated on the ground was a flat stone slab with eight bowls of steaming opaque liquid. It was the smell that drew the young man further into the cave, hypnotizing him. For a brief second he forgot about his fear and pain.

"Food?" he murmured out loud to no one.

"It's yours," came a calm, soothing voice from behind. The young man whipped around ready to smash anything and everything.

The young man saw the old hiker from earlier in the day perched on a rock outcropping drinking from a bowl, "What are you doing here, you donkey!"

Unfazed, the old hiker continued, "I didn't go too far after I left because you didn't look well. I watched as the wind caught you off guard. You cracked your skull pretty hard. When I realized you weren't dead from your fall, I knew you would need some nourishment and shelter so I made soup," the old man said pointing to the eight bowls. "They're all yours. Each is a favorite recipe I've been working on for years. Eat up before they get cold."

The young man started crying and dropped his staff. He was too tired and hurting to be angry or resist the old hiker's kindness. He wondered again if he might be hallucinating but then convinced himself that if he were, he didn't care. He knelt down on a small rug next to the rock and picked up the first bowl of soup and devoured the broth. He began rocking back and forth, moaning in ecstasy as the soup dripped from the corners of his mouth down his beard. Each bowl filled his belly with goodness and warmth.

Then the young man had a queer thought as he scanned the interior of the small cavern, "Why have I never seen this place before? It's a perfect shelter." The only sounds in the small cave were the crackling of fire and the sound of the young man slurping from the bowls.

"There is a cot on the floor in the corner if you would like to rest," the old hiker noted.

The young man finished the eighth bowl and slumped back on the ground, staring at the rock ceiling. After a long pause he spoke, "Thank you. I am eternally grateful for your gift. Why did you do this for me after how rude I was to you?"

"To celebrate you," the old hiker smiled.

"Celebrate me for what?"

"Your new freedom."

"My freedom? I'm not a prisoner. I came here on my own free will and can leave this mountain any time I want. Your talk is madness!"

"I saw you today walking around and around in circles. From the look of things, you've been here a while. When you told me your dilemma, I replied with a simple answer. You could not accept my simple explanation. You were blinded by your anger and sent me away. When I saw the gust of wind, I knew it was The Universe or "mountain gods," as you call them, loving you. She blinded you with tears. She placed that rock under your foot so you would stumble. She ordered the wind to rise from the valley and sweep up the side of the mountain because you needed a little shove in the right direction. You no longer trust yourself. You will not listen to reason. But The Universe isn't put off so easily. She still loves you and will continue to place stones and strangers in your path. I am simply following my heart and playing my part in your drama. You must once again return to trusting yourself or you will end up walking in circles the rest of your life, trying to solve unsolvable riddles."

The young man listened but did not speak.

"You have much life left to live. It's time to get down from this mountain of isolation."

"Thank you," was all the young man could manage. The two men sat in silence listening to the rain and ice pelt the bare mountain.

"I wish I could say my motives are altruistic," the old man finally spoke with a mischievous grin.

"What do you mean? Why are you helping me then?"

"Because you are me. I am you. I am only one of your futures. I am the you that leaves this mountain. Those gods you speak of have given me a glimpse into our life, and it is so full of happiness and love and joy. This life of isolation, the one you inhabit now, is empty, sad, lonely. I understand it has not been all bad for you. Those splendid sunrises and glorious sunsets we have witnessed are spectacular. The wholesome landscape after a heavy snow or watching a grizzly momma tend her cubs. Life down from this mountain is not without its own sorrow. I don't mean to patronize. You've been intimate with misery." The old man looked at the eight empty bowls stacked on the stone table. "You never have to leave this mountain. It is your choice," and with a tender smile and a wink added, "but I would highly recommend it."

S.T.A.R.

Subconscious Temperament +
Automatic Reactions

Template Instructions

The following pages contain two s.t.a.r. diagrams. The first is an example of a completed emblem. You will need the following information to complete your own s.t.a.r. diagram.

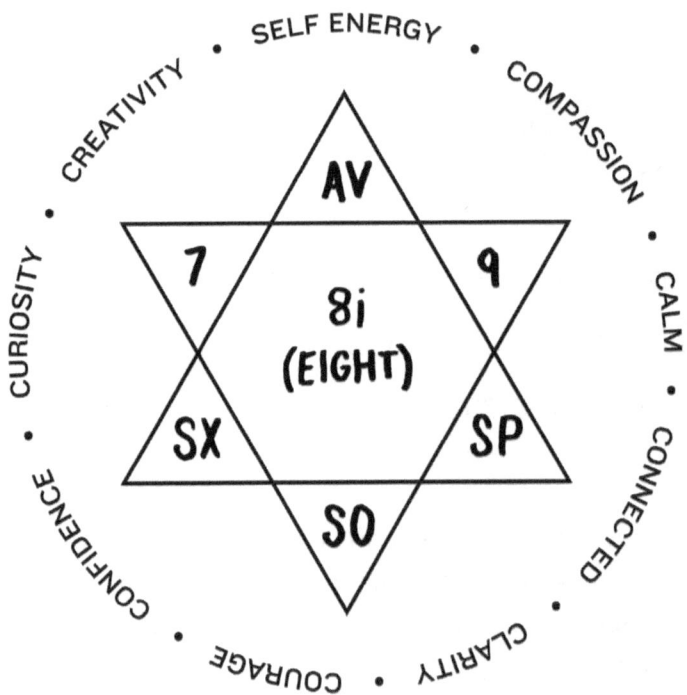

1. Write your Enneagram type/number in the center along with your style of rejuvenation: Introvert (i), Extrovert (x) or Ambivert (a).

2. Your Attachment Style – Secure (S), Anxious (AX) or Avoidant (AV). In the example above Avoidant [AV] is the attachment style.

3. You will need your Enneagram "wings," which are the two numbers on each side of your primary personality type. 1 (9 & 2), 2 (1 & 3), 3 (2 & 4), 4 (3 & 5), 5 (4 & 6), 6 (5 & 7), 7 (6 & 8), 8 (7 & 9), 9 (8 & 1). In the example above, #7 & #9 are the wings.

4. You will need your two primary Enneagram Instincts. The three instincts are Social (SO), Sexual (1-to-1 Bonding) (SX) and Self Preservation (SP). Typically, two are primary and secondary and the third is a blind spot. In the example above, Sexual (SX) is primary and Self Preservation (SP) is secondary.

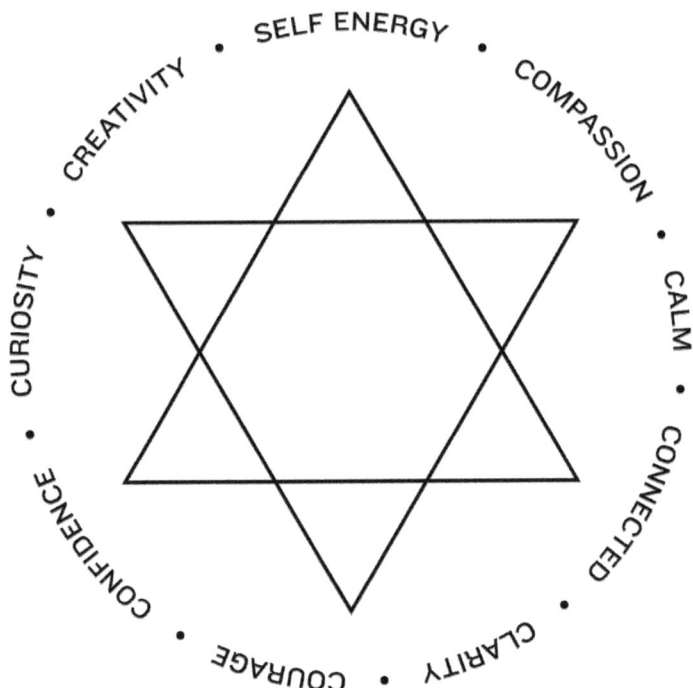

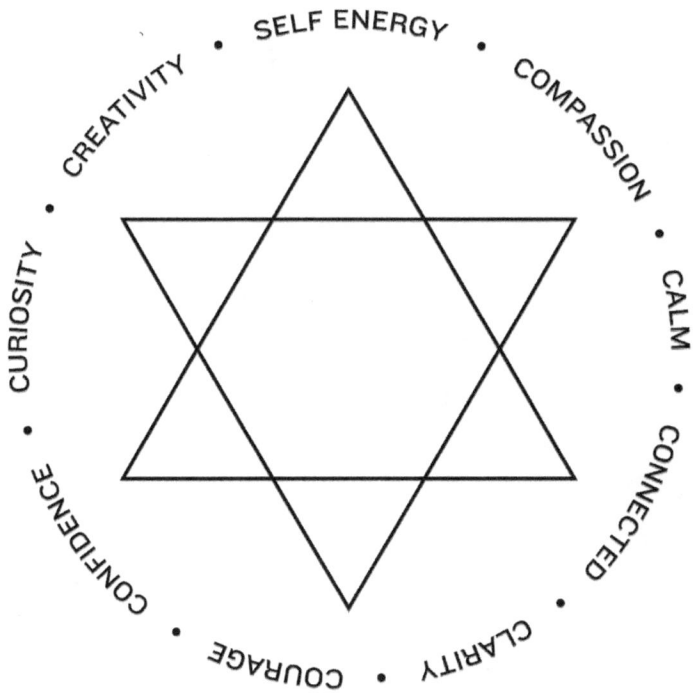

ABOUT THE AUTHOR

Reb Buxton is a human behavior expert. He received his Master's in Counseling Psychology from The Seattle School of Theology & Psychology in Seattle, Washington. He has dedicated the last 15+ years to working with children, families, couples and individuals helping them heal from past trauma and build healthy relationships. It is his passion to help alleviate unnecessary suffering and help people find authentic happiness.

To find out more about Reb and his work please visit:

RebBuxton.com

BeingHappy.blog

TheFlowFarm.com

www.ingramcontent.com/pod-product-compliance
Lightning Source LLC
Chambersburg PA
CBHW020359080526
44584CB00014B/1088